Individualizing Physical Education

CRITERION MATERIALS

Second Edition

Dorothy Zakrajsek, PhD
The University of Idaho

Lois A. Carnes, MED
Solon City Schools, Solon, Ohio

Human Kinetics Publishers, Inc.
Champaign, Illinois

Library of Congress Cataloging-in-Publication Data
Zakrajsek, Dorothy.
    Individualizing physical education.

    Rev. ed. of: Learning experiences. c1981.
    Bibliography: p.
    1. Physical education and training—Study and
teaching.   2. Individualized instruction.   I. Carnes,
Lois. II. Zakrajsek, Dorothy.   Learning experiences.
III. Title.
GV363.Z26 1986   613.7'07   85-27120
ISBN 0-87322-045-5

Developmental Editor: Sue Ingels Mauck
Production Director: Ernie Noa
Typesetter: Lewis Publishing
Text Layout: Lezli Harris
Cover Design and Layout: Jack Davis
Printed By: United Graphics

ISBN: 0-87322-045-5

Printed in the United States of America

10 9 8 7 6 5 4 3 2 1

Human Kinetics Publishers, Inc.
Box 5076, Champaign, IL 61820

Dedication

This book is dedicated to our children:

Michael, Thomas and Mary Jo Zakrajsek
Russell and Stacey Carnes

Contents

Preface

Individualizing Physical Education: Criterion Materials is a text designed primarily for physical education majors and nonmajors (classroom teachers) enrolled in teacher preparation courses at the undergraduate level. The focus of our teacher preparation spans upper elementary through senior high school with more application on the junior high curriculum. We selected the following twelve activity units which are generally taught in the aforementioned curriculum: Selected Fundamental Skills, Rhythmic Gymnastics, Tumbling, Gymnastics, Track and Field, Badminton, Tennis, Basketball, Flag Football, Soccer, Softball, and Volleyball. Several Task Learning Experiences were constructed for each skill associated with the activity. These tasks provide the instructor or student with content or actual problems that guide the learner through the execution of each skill. The tasks are arranged sequentially so that the learner can progress from a basic skill level to a complete, well-executed performance of that skill. These tasks may be presented to the students using various methodological approaches.

In addition to the Task Learning Experiences, each skill within the units provides a statement of Purpose as well as a thorough but brief Skill Analysis of the skill. The Purpose aids the student or teacher in establishing a learning goal prior to execution of the skill. Likewise, the Skill Analysis provides the instructor or student with a quick overview of the components of the skill (example — body position, follow-through, etc.) prior to instruction and thus facilitates later execution of the skill.

While the twelve activity units provide the teacher with content or material to be taught, the units are purposely preceded by four chapters which give meaning and direction to the user. The pedagogy chapter (chapter one) reviews several commonly accepted teaching practices in physical education. Because of the popularity of Muska Mosston's seven teaching styles, we have examined each in accordance with task application.

An organizational chapter (chapter two) describes practical alternatives for planning class sessions utilizing tasks. Some of these forms of class organization include grouping, station work, and a learning center approach. Additionally, safety guidelines, task card models, and specific applications for utilizing the task learning experiences are presented. Since our text cannot list all task possibilities for each unit of activity, we have included a section on Task Preparation in chapter two in order to encourage teachers to create additional tasks.

Chapter three gives a brief description of individualized education and various approaches as a backdrop for the authors' own model of task strategy — Supervised Task Programming.

Chapter four presents two different approaches for using task learning experiences. The first model arranges tasks into mini-units of instruction for middle school students. The second model is a senior high learning package on badminton. Both applications are complete with detailed procedures for classroom adoption.

Since task teaching is the emphasis of the text, it should be noted that we have taken one of Muska Mosston's seven identifiable styles of teaching, Task, (from his text *Teaching Physical Education*) and expanded it to include both a teaching and learning strategy. Task teaching boasts several advantages. It provides the student with a clearly defined learning goal. It allows the student to proceed at his/her own rate. It motivates the student to complete a goal which has immediate evaluative feedback. It frees the teacher to work independently of the whole class and allows observation, analyzation, and evaluation of student performance on a one-to-one relationship. In an educational era that encourages individualized learning, task teaching initiates the process for developing an individualized program.

In conclusion, our major goal is to have systematically constructed a sequential set of learning experiences for the most common sports and activities used in the upper elementary through senior high school and thus provide a practical guide or comprehensive curriculum for physical education instructors already in the field or for those who are preparing to teach. The utilization and application of our text will enhance a physical education teacher's, student teacher's, or classroom teacher's program and provide an excellent source of content and methodology.

The authors are particularly grateful to Janet L. Woods for her support and help with several aspects of the text. We also extend our appreciation to the Ohio students at Solon Junior High, Kent State University School, Hudson Junior High School; to their teachers, Janet Woods, Willis Woods, David Toothaker, Becky Fox, and Kathy Leighton; to Ernest Carnes and Carl Zakraysek for the photography; and to Mark Gorman and Kent Smith for the line drawings.

D.Z.
L.C.

Section 1

ONE

Pedagogical Strategies with Task Application

LEARNING

Teaching and learning are analogous to the flip sides of the same coin. Courses in educational psychology and pedagogy rarely deal with teaching without devoting considerable time and space to learning or learning theory. Teaching purports to direct some overt behavior for the intended purpose of learning which makes it illogical to isolate the process of teaching from the intended process of learning. On the other hand, learning doesn't necessarily preclude teaching. All of us have learned much of what we know by means other than having been taught in a formalized setting.

Learning something is generally followed by a change in behavior; thinking, feeling, doing. Learning is inferred when the learner performs some behavior that wasn't observable or measurable before being placed in a learning situation. The principal means for learning are visual (reading and seeing), aural (listening), and physical (doing). Learning that, learning to, and learning how to are modes of learning that imply cognitive, affective, and motor responses or changes in behavior.

CONDITIONS OF LEARNING

Several variables influence learning. Hudgins (1971) believes that recognizing three conditions under which learning occurs is vital to a concept of teaching. He calls attention to physical, school, and individual factors. The physical factor, growth and development, is fixed and, therefore, subject to minimal, if any, controls. In other words, the developmental level of a student is a situational given in any classroom; and since classrooms are made up of several students, several different stages of development will be represented. Because of this heterogeneity of maturation levels, it is imperative that the physical education teacher plan learning activities with each pupil in mind. For example, some intermediate grade pupils are not physiologically able to shoot free throws using regulation basketballs, standing at the free throw line, and shooting at ten foot high baskets. This activity, if pursued and continued, will frustrate those learners since failure is most assuredly programmed. Recognizing physiological differences might result in allowing for the use of different sized and weighted balls, allowing for different shooting distances from the basket, lowering the height of some baskets, changing the time duration of the activity, and so forth. Secondly, Hudgins contends that school variables, a physical location and a host of curricular and instructional resources are essential for learning. Physical educators have always been aware of the effect that indoor and outdoor facilities have on learning and ought to be aware that long lines and limited equipment reduce learning opportunities. Without different weighted, sized, and shaped balls, it would be difficult to study the relationships of mass, velocity, trajectory, speed, and distance.

Finally, he identifies individual pupil variables as motivation, learning styles, and personality needs. While these three factors are tacitly accepted as conditions necessary to learning, they are most commonly ignored in application. Too many physical education classrooms foster and perpetuate a method of teaching that supports a singular learning concept for all students based on one kind of motivation, one style of learning, and one set of learning needs. Otherwise, our classrooms would be satiated with examples of methodological approaches that attended to individual learning differences.

While perhaps the solution appears simplistic, the problem is, indeed, complex. Even though several textbooks and papers have been written on motor learning, there is still much to be learned about the nature of learning, the learner, and the process of teaching. Suffice it to note here some commonly accepted principles of learning which ought to be incorporated into the mainstream of physical education lesson planning.

- Learning is individualistic; each learner has a different learning cycle.
- Learning should be commensurate with the developmental level of the learner.
- Learning is best accomplished when the learner wants to learn.
- Learning is more meaningful when it can be linked with application.
- Learning occurs more rapidly when the learning situation is satisfying to the learner.
- Learning is facilitated when the learner has a clearly established goal in mind.

- Learning is more rapid when the goal is meaningful and has merit for the learner.
- Learning is more effective when feedback or knowledge of results is provided.

Within the conditions of learning must be considered pupil ability to learn or comprehend, pupil perseverance and motivation to learn, the quality of instruction, the availability of materials and resources for learning, and the opportunity to learn. Obviously, the student who lacks ability and interest, encounters poor teaching, is provided limited materials, and is given few chances for subject matter interaction is doomed, at best, to minimal learning. In summary, all learning is enhanced and proceeds more effectively when the conditions for learning are maximized.

TEACHING STRATEGIES

Methodological processes ascribed to the teaching of physical education have been referred to as teaching styles, techniques, methods, procedures, and, in a broader sense, have included organization and administration. Teaching strategies, a more current term in pedagogical vocabulary, will, for our purposes, encompass those variables in the teaching-learning environment which can be controlled, managed, and manipulated by the teacher for the purpose of facilitating learning. The term "strategy" connotes advance determination of a goal, planning for goal attainment, a delivery system, and assessment of goal achievement. More specifically, teaching strategies refer to the deliberate management of instruction and are directed toward the accomplishment of predetermined learning outcomes.

While we would all agree that the teacher cannot learn for the student, we do recognize that the quantity and quality of what students learn and their motivation to learn are substantially influenced by the behavior of the teacher. In recent years teaching behavior has been systematically analyzed for both descriptive and prescriptive purposes. The presence or absence of certain teaching behaviors has aided in defining direct and indirect approaches to teaching. Direct, a teacher centered method, and indirect, a student centered method, are predicated upon certain beliefs and assumptions about the teaching-learning process. A closer examination of each reveals the basic differences.

TEACHER-CENTERED METHOD

Teacher-centered or direct teaching can be likened to an act of one way communication. Simply stated, the teacher transmits knowledge by some means to the learner. Perhaps the following illustration more clearly expresses that meaning:

SENDER	.... MESSAGE	.......CHANNEL	..RECEIVER
or	↓	↓	↓	↓
TEACHER	.. SUBJECT MATTER	... METHOD	.. LEARNER
or	↓	↓	↓	↓
....WHO	.... WHAT	...........HOW	..... WHOM

Figure 1.1

In this model, the teacher plays a direct role, a role expectation popularly viewed and defended by many. The focus of educational development is on the teacher and subject matter. The teacher orders and sequences the content, determines the learning experiences, organizes and arranges the learning environment, and delivers the subject matter. This method is associated with reception learning which stresses the deliberate organization of subject matter in such a way that meaningful tasks are hierarchically arranged so that learning is incremental.

As such, the teacher is the subject or active doer while the learner is represented in the objective case or as a passive receiver. This method has been critically described as a "pouring in" rather than "bringing out" process. In physical education jargon, it is commonly referred to as "tell 'em, drill 'em, and play 'em."

Instruction identified with this method is commonly characterized by a teacher who decides what students should learn, what will be taught, how much, and at what level of difficulty. Additionally, he/she determines time allotments, arrangement of equipment, formation of students, use of instructional resources, methods of presentation, and standards of evaluation. The quality of teacher-centeredness evokes a "sameness." The same thing is taught to all students at the same time in the same way, and the expectations are that students will practice the same thing in the same way at the same pace for the same amount of time and be evaluated by the same performance criteria.

Advocates of the direct teaching approach contend that class organization, discipline, time efficiency, pupil security, safety, and general teaching and learning effectiveness are better attended to when autonomously controlled and administered by the teacher. Arguments, commonly advanced by the critics, suggest that the passive role of the students detracts from the joys of learning; limits student initiative, curiosity, creativity, and intellectual ability; and makes him/her dependent upon the teacher as the source of knowledge.

LEARNER-CENTERED METHOD

Education in the sixties and seventies has emphasized student-centered learning or an indirect approach to teaching. The focus for educational development is on the student. Labels such as humanism, personalization, individualization, group-centered, student-centered, democratic, discovery, and problem solving have highlighted an attempt to break away from the conventional teacher-dominated classroom. Research on teacher education is replete with programs and practices that promote greater student participation in and responsibility for the process of learning and thinking. Under this method, the student is no longer relegated to a receivership role but is encouraged to participate actively in the determination of what to learn, how much, and under what conditions.

If sameness depicts teacher-centered instruction, then differences represent student-centered teaching. Pupil differences in abilities, interests, maturation, attitudes, skills, and goals are rationalized as foundational for developing teaching behaviors that promote inquiry and independent learning styles in students.

Individualizing learning is viewed from two perspectives: product and process. The first is directed toward content mastery or performance achievement. The teacher is portrayed as a director of learning activities. Instructional considerations stress the components of self-paced supervised study, i.e., goal selection, attainment of criterion-referenced performance standards, use of instructional media, frequent and positive reinforcement, and learner-to-teacher relationship. Students are given substantial decision-making powers in tailoring their own instructional programs, which is espoused as a major factor in self-motivated and self-initiated learning. Programs commonly associated here, to name a few, include programmed learning, individualization, personalization, competency-based, and independent study.

The second pedagogical strategy focuses on learning processes and is characterized by discovery techniques. Problems or learning tasks are constructed by the teacher and presented to the student for solution. Content is arranged in such a way that only through a process of inquiry can the student reach a solution. According to proponents of discovery learning, it is the act of solving that generates cognitive activity and excitement which they claim as an indispensable condition for learning, retention, and transferability. The role of the teacher as described by Hudgins (1971, p. 32) is one of "a mediator between the learner and the phenomenon about which he is to learn." Exploration, experimentation, guided discovery, and problem solving are methods generally listed under discovery techniques.

Teacher-centered and student-centered methods both require good teachers who know how to alter instructional behaviors, procedures, processes, and activities in order to facilitate learning. Teachers must order, structure, and sequence meaningful learning tasks that beget measurable gains in levels of thinking and doing whether teacher-presented or learner-discovered. A poor teacher will produce poor learning regardless of the favored approach. The best teachers, in our opinion, will incorporate the merits of both approaches.

SYSTEMS APPROACH TO TEACHING

The nature of a systems approach and its applicability to the instructional process will be briefly reviewed here. The operational components of a systemic model closely parallel those of product individualization. A systems approach is also behavioristically formulated with a content mastery its intended goal. A system is defined as the sum of its interrelated parts of which the purpose or system output is the attainment of a specific goal. According to Banathy (1968), an instructional system deals with the processes and functions which are sequentially structured in the learning environment in order to facilitate mastery of specific learning tasks.

The design of a system model for instruction usually stresses the following progressive components:

- Formulate specific learning outcomes.
- Develop tests for measuring learning outcomes.
- Assess entry capabilities of the learner.
- Identify learning tasks.
- Select learning materials and resources to aid in achieving the learning goal.
- Provide feedback to learner.
- Regulate the system and make adjustments after evaluating the effectiveness of the system output.

The success of a system approach rests with the resourcefulness of the teacher. Since prepared learning materials in physical education have been somewhat scarce, the teacher is left to his/her own inventiveness. The next chapter describes a procedure for writing task learning experiences while chapters 3 through 14 provide task learning experiences specific to a number of individual and team activities.

DIRECT INSTRUCTION

Direct instruction has been described as a concept about teaching rather than a method. The title should not be confused with direct teaching or direct teaching styles mentioned earlier in this chapter, although similarities may be noted.

An accumulation of research on teaching has identified several process variables (those behaviors that describe what goes on in the teaching-learning setting) that have related well with achievement and attitude variables across several subject areas. A synthesis of these process variables that contributed to learning gains resulted in the term *Direct Instruction* (Becker et al., 1981; Berliner & Rosenshine, 1977; Gage, 1978; Good, 1979; Graham & Heimerer, 1981; Rosenshine, 1979).

Characteristics of direct instruction that are commonly cited by the above researchers are associated with enthusiastic and highly motivated teachers. Teaching is described as deliberate, businesslike, active, and task-oriented. Much attention is given to time-on-task or academic learning time. The teacher sets and articulates learning goals; structures learning; actively assesses and monitors student progress; focuses on learning and accountability; plans for active involvement and on-task behaviors; uses criterion materials; provides close supervision and immediate and academic feedback; maintains high performance expectations; allows all to experience success; uses modeling behavior; employs whole groups when teaching new content; asks factual and concrete questions; and, finally, is approachable and creates a warm, "I care about you" atmosphere.

Direct Instruction was more tersely defined by Fielding et al. (1983) as follows:

> *Direct instruction is a tightly structured approach to teaching, in which each step in the learning process is clearly articulated. In direct instruction students are shown explicitly how to perform given skills, receive extensive practice in applying these skills, and receive frequent feedback on their progress toward skill mastery. Direct instruction lessons are designed, moreover, such that the learner experiences a high degree of success during each phase of the lesson (p.287).*

MOSSTON: AN OVERVIEW WITH TASK APPLICATION

Mosston's (1966) spectrum of teaching styles describes and analyzes seven methods for teaching physical education. His styles are theoretically based in minimal and maximal potentials for student development — physically, socially, emotionally, and intellectually. The range or styles (command, task, reciprocal, group, individual program, guided discovery, and problem solving) are developmentally sequenced with command promising the least and problem solving the most.

He partitions these styles into direct teaching (command through individual program) and indirect teaching (guided discovery and problem solving). The direct teaching lesson is characterized by explanation, demonstration (sometimes given together or reversed), execution, and evaluation. The difference among the direct styles is noted in the execution phase. In indirect methodology, explanation and demonstration are substituted with problem setting and cueing.

For Mosston, the ultimate goal of education is to produce an independent thinker capable of decision making, inquiry, problem solving, and creativity. To accomplish this, he relies upon alternative teaching styles to guide students toward this end. His seven styles are briefly described and each is followed by a task application. For a complete understanding of Mosston's work, the reader is directed to study the original text.

Command:

The command style is easily recognized because all students are doing the same thing at the same time. There is little flexibility, little student input, and little recognition of individual differences. Whole class and/or squads mark the usual grouping pattern. After the teacher explains what to do and shows a level of intended perform- ance, the class is dispersed to practice under the control of the teacher. The teacher signals the commencement of practice, sets the duration of activity, and issues evaluations, corrections, and praise to the whole class or individuals.

Task Application—Command:

Tasks #1 and #2 from forehand drive, tennis.
1. Stand sideways to wall, backboard, or fence and hit 10 dropped balls with open palm of hand.
2. Repeat Task #1 using a tennis racket.
    Class of 30 is organized into 10 groups of three and is indoors. The teacher demonstrates dropping the ball and hitting it with the open palm while explaining the mechanics. The execution phase might look like the following:
* Teacher directs first 10 to a line and says, "Ready, drop, back- swing, contact, shift your weight and follow through."
* "Get another ball, Ready, . . . " Repeat until all three balls have been hit.
* "Retrieve all balls and go to the end of your line. Second person up to the line. Ready, drop, etc."
* After a teacher determined practice duration, the teacher calls the class together to talk about or evaluate the results. The teacher introduces the use of the racket, demonstrates forehand grip, and explains and demonstrates the forehand drive from a side position. Included is an explanation about force production and the advan- tage of a longer lever. Students are directed to move farther away from the wall and the teacher commences activity.
* "First person, ready, drop . . . etc."

Task:

Task is a direct teaching style that attends to some student differen- ces and needs. Following explanation and demonstration, the class is presented with a task, a series of tasks, or a range of tasks. During the developmental or execution phase, students are permitted some control in setting their pace, duration, quality, and quantity of perform- ance. A major benefit for the teacher is the freedom to move around for individual or small group observation, analyzation, and correction. There is a freer atmosphere and some opportunity for student inter- action as well as student-to-teacher. Small groups, partners, and individuals are the usual groupings, although the whole class could be utilized.

Soccer drill under command style

Task Application—Task:

Tasks #4 and #6 from trapping, soccer.
1. In partners, A rolls the ball to B who traps with the sole of foot. Repeat 10 times reversing roles.
2. Repeat Task #1 using the inside of leg trap.
3. Repeat Task #1 using inside of both legs or front of both legs.
4. Repeat Task #1, but partner calls the kind of trap when releasing the ball.
5. Repeat Task #4, but partner kicks the ball instead of rolling.

After teacher explanation and demonstration of these three methods of trapping a soccer ball, the class is presented with the tasks. Students are grouped into partners. Under this method, pupils select an area of the field, start on their own, choose their own distances, determine the speed of the throw, and work relatively free from the rest of the class. The teacher walks around and gives individual help, encouragement, and positive reinforcement.

Reciprocal:

The reciprocal method emphasizes student-to-student relationships. The organizational structure is partners. One performs a skill while the other acts as an observer, corrector, and reinforcer, and then the roles are reversed. The teacher never corrects the performer but rather reestablishes performance criteria with the observer.

The imperative necessary to the success of reciprocal teaching is in student understanding of performance criteria. During the explanation/demonstration phase, the teacher must communicate the checkpoints for skill mastery. In accepting observer responsibilities, the observer internalizes skill information that aids his/her own learning process as it relates to that skill. It should be noted that the observer cannot be a part of the activity of the performer but must remain unencumbered to complete his/her observer role. Again, there is flexibility in pacing, duration, and interaction.

Task Application—Reciprocal:
Tasks #1 and #11 from centering, flag football.
1. In partners, A assumes a centering position for a set back hike and B evaluates the position according to the skill analysis. Reverse.
11. In partners, A assumes a centering position for a T-formation hike. B evaluates the position according to the skill analysis. Reverse.

After explanation/demonstration, the class is organized into partners. Task cards with skill analysis and tasks are provided. The teacher is free to observe and assist the observer if needed.

Peer checking skill analysis—reciprocal style

Small Group:
The small group style builds on the reciprocal method. Instead of working in twos, the groups are expanded to three or four with defined roles of performer, observer, or two observers, and recorder.

Task Application—Small Group:
Task #12 from sprint, track and field.
12. In groups of four, combine the crouch start with a 25-yard acceleration three times and record each. A is the sprinter, B evalu-

Peers analyzing punting form—reciprocal style

Students engaged in small group method

ates the crouch start and acceleration, C times and records, and D gives starting commands. Rotate roles.

Following teacher explanation/demonstration, the class is organized into groups of four and dispersed to complete the assignment. The teacher moves among the groups and continues to observe and assist the observer if needed.

Individual Program:

The teacher presents learning packages that describe performance objectives, learning tasks, evaluation criteria, and instructional resources. The student assumes the responsibility for determining his own learning. Usually the student will contract to complete a given number of performance behaviors at a specified standard of achievement. Each student has his/her own program which might be duplicated or overlapped with others. Pretesting and posttesting might be included as well as teacher consultation in setting a program.

Task Application—Individual Program:

Tasks: All tennis skills from tennis.
All tennis skill tasks are listed as well as the skill analysis for each. Instructional resources might be added which could include library book references, films, loops, video tape replay, televised matches, etc. The student selects the number of learning tasks, chooses the level of proficiency and agrees to complete his/her program within a specified time period.

Guided Discovery:

Guided discovery is an indirect method of teaching which proceeds from the general to the specific. The teacher arranges a sequence of problems which, when solved, lead to a particular response. When solving a problem or problems, the learner is obliged to make cognitive responses as well as motor. It is during this process, the act of discovering, the figuring out, that the student benefits most. The learner is never given the expected outcome or a modeling behavior. The student isn't told or shown the best place to contact a ball when kicking for distance or height but learns to discover this through solving problem tasks which are teacher structured. Guided discovery infers teacher assistance through questioning, cueing, and designing steps or additional steps that will aid the student in reaching the planned learning goal. Reinforcement is operationally linked to guided discovery and is given after each successful response to a problem or sub problem.

Task Application—Guided Discovery:

Tasks #21 and 22 from dribbling, basketball.
21.   One-on-One. In partners stand in a stationary position. Stand about two feet apart and face-to-face. A dribbles while B tries to deflect or steal the ball. Dribble high/low, fast/slow, eyes on ball/eyes on opponent, finger tip striking/whole palm striking. Do not make body contact. Reverse. Discuss what you discovered about ball control.
22.   One-on-One. In partners move through space. A dribbles the ball through space while B tries to deflect or steal the ball. Dribble close/loose, fast/slow, high/medium/low, straight

pathways/zigzag, forward/sideways. Do not make body contact. Discuss what you discovered about maintaining ball possession and control.

22.1   Is it easier for the defense to take away a close or loose dribble? Why?

22.2   Is it easier for the defense to take away a fast or slow dribble? Why?

22.3   What is the best height for dribbling when you are closely guarded? Why?

22.4   How can you use your body to help maintain possession of the ball?

Problem Solving:

Problem solving is another indirect teaching style that allows for individualization of responses or solutions. The teacher sets a problem(s) which evokes a solution(s). Differentiation of responses is expected because the problem is designed to elicit many responses. Problem solving differs from guided discovery in that a single problem can have several correct solutions whereas in guided discovery, the end result is one final solution. Problems can be individually or group posed. Positive reinforcement and frequent feedback are essential teacher behaviors.

Task Application—Problem Solving:

Tasks #8 and #9 from deflagging, flag football.

8. In two teams of four players each, devise a play where the offensive team will center and pass or center and run for yardage. The defensive team will attempt to deflag the ball carrier or deflect the pass. Allow three plays per team before changing from offense to defense. Rotate positions within the team.

9. Repeat Task #8 by adding more rules and scoring.

MOVEMENT EDUCATION APPROACH

During the 1960s elementary physical education programs integrated a new approach which has come to be known as movement education. Movement education is the segment of a child's education that provides the skills to meet the demands of any movement task with which he/she is confronted. In order to teach the child these various motor skills, movement education encompasses a systematic body of knowledge as well as a specific methodological approach. The movement education approach basically employs a child-centered, indirect methodology. With reference to Mosston's classifications of teaching methods, the two most widely used in movement education are guided discovery and problem solving. However, proponents of the movement education approach have advocated an additional indirect method of teaching not described by Mosston. The term "movement exploration" has been used to define a form of experimentation in which the child "explores" how and where his/her body can move. The teacher does not propose that the child arrive at one or several problematical solutions following the exploration. Instead, the end result ought to be the child's greater awareness of his/her movement capabilitities. This methodological approach should not be interpreted as a period of free play since the teacher still carefully plans the environment and provides stimuli for the exploration.

The use of indirect methodology in a movement education program has advantages for both the learner and the teacher. The learner is able to progress at his/her own rate and at his/her own level of ability as he/she seeks a solution to the questions or tasks proposed by the teacher. This also promotes an atmosphere of creativity which contributes to the improvement of a student's self-image and personal awareness. Opportunities for success are provided for all students which impact on affective goals and personal satisfaction. The noncompetitive nature of the program is likewise very conducive to learning

In using the indirect method, the teacher benefits by becoming a facilitator of knowledge rather than a manipulator of what the child learns. This provides the teacher with time to aid each learner individually as he/she proceeds without direct teacher control. Teacher demonstrations likewise become passe.

Although supporters of movement education advocate the use of indirect methodology, the direct methods are often an integral part of the approach. In reference to Mosston's classifications, there are situations when command, task, reciprocal, small group or individualized methodology are applicable. A student may at times need the teacher's direct instruction for action through a command. Likewise, the teacher may decide upon a specific task to be performed by the student on his/her own. Partner feedback through reciprocal observation of performance is congruent with the movement approach as well as is small group reinforcement. Finally, an individualized method clearly provides opportunity for utilization of a self-motivated program of learning. The learner participates in his/her own decision-making and self-analysis.

Task learning experiences can be employed as a unique teaching tool within a movement education program. Thus, their utilization is advantageous in movement education. The following are set forth as a sampling of open-ended, indirect task learning experiences that might be incorporated into movement education lessons.

Selected Fundamental Skills
Throw
- Throw 10 balls as far as possible while standing behind a line (overhand throw). How should the feet be placed to keep from losing balance? What foot position helped the body get momentum for a far throw?
- Throw 10 balls as far as possible from a run (overhand throw). Did the balls go farther when throwing from a run or a stand? Why do you think this happened?

Catch
- In partners, A tosses 10 balls to B. (reverse) What hand positions did you find to be the best for catching the ball?
- In partners, A tosses five balls to B. (reverse) How should the feet and body be placed to best receive the ball? What foot position gave you the most balance for catching? If the ball were thrown with more force, would the placement of the feet be more important?

Track and Field

Standing Long Jump
- Take 10 jumps from a stand behind a line. How can the body move in order to get momentum before the jump?
- Take five jumps from a stand behind a line and try to jump over a string 1½ feet high. Does increasing the height of the jump help to increase the distance?

Volleyball

Overhand Volley
- In partners, volley the ball for five minutes over a rope stretched high across the gym. How should the hands strike the ball to volley the ball high in the air?
- In partners, volley the ball for five minutes over a net. How can the body move or what can the body do in order to get more force and height in the volley?

TWO

Organizational Strategies for Task Application

Task is both a teaching and learning strategy that relies upon teacher implementation and direction while employing a student/subject matter relationship. The educational rewards accrued from implementing task programming are many, but they are contingent upon teacher commitment and teacher/student interpersonal relationships.

Task becomes a teaching strategy when the teacher designs a series of tasks and organizes the class to accommodate teaching behaviors. The use of tasks frees the teacher from the constraints of whole class instruction so that he/she can engage in individual or small group observation, analyzation, prescription, correction, and reinforcement. This process personalizes the communication between the teacher and student which promotes a healthy and caring relationship.

Task becomes a learning strategy when the emphasis for learning shifts to the learner. Task learning experiences give the learner direction and meaning for practicing skills. Since tasks generally provide a set of behavioral expectations, the learner experiences less confusion about what he/she is expected to do. Standards of achievement contained within the task provide immediate feedback about performance. The accomplishment of a task is reinforcing and rewarding to the learner which can motivate continued performance growth. The use of tasks relies upon learner acceptance of some of the responsibility for learning, thereby, reducing teacher dependence.

ORGANIZING STRATEGIES

Task programming provides the teacher with several alternatives when planning the class session.

Grouping

Tasks can be utilized with various grouping patterns: individual, partners, small group, and whole class as well as homogeneous or heterogeneous grouping.

Selection

A continuum of teacher influence from direct to indirect is determined by who selects the tasks. Teacher selection might focus on the quantitative (duration or repetitions) or qualitative (assessment of skill) aspects of development; while student selection might be motivated by interest, challenge, or achievement either quantitatively or qualitatively. Selection might be determined cooperatively between the teacher and the student. Tasks can be selected sequentially and arranged for progressive skill acquisition (i.e., student performs tasks 1 through 8) or can be randomly chosen (i.e., student performs tasks 3, 7, and 9 from a list of tasks). Selection can also be comprehensive by choosing tasks from a number of skills within an activity (i.e., student performs a specified task from dribbling, goal shooting, and guarding in basketball).

Stations

Task programming can be utilized through station or circuit planning. Stations can be arranged to accommodate:
- Progressive skill acquisition (tasks at each successive station become more difficult).
- Cross section of skills within an activity (volleyball tasks for the underhand serve at one station, set pass at another, and spiking at a third).
- Skills with common movement patterns (overhand throw, tennis serve, and forward pass).
- Equipment (tasks within a rhythmic gymnastics lesson could employ ropes at one station, balls at another, and hoops at a third).
- Diversity of skill ability (a range of tasks at each station with students working on those tasks commensurate with their ability).

The above stations can be modified by employing such factors as:
- Variable repetitions.
- Rotation after set duration of time.
- Rotation only after successful completion.
- Student selection of tasks.

Methodology

Various methodological approaches can be used with task programming. Direct and indirect styles of teaching can be applied which were discussed in chapter 1. Task delivery can be

STATION #2
TASKS-PASSING-FOOTBALL

1. In partners, pass back and forth concentrating on the mechanics of passing, control and producing a spiral motion.

2. Repeat task #1 increasing the distance. Concentrate on producing force.

3. In partners, A passes to B who is moving away from A in a forward direction. Repeat until successful 3 out of 5 times. Reverse.

4. Repeat task #3 with B moving a few strides forward _____ to the left for a pass. Repeat _____ of 5 times. Reverse.

5. Repe _____ cutting to the right.

6. Repe _____ cuts.

Task charts describe performance expectations

accomplished through the use of task cards and instructional resources. Task cards usually describe learning experiences and allow for a record of completion and assessment. For example, see figures 2.1, 2.2, and 2.3. Other instructional resources generally used for task delivery include transparencies, charts, and listening tapes.

Individualization

Task programming can serve the development of an individualized program or an individualized instruction as one of its intended goals. Skill tasks can be used for:

- Preassessment: determining student proficiency or entry skill level.
- Goal-setting: identifying student objectives.
- Contracting: choosing to fulfill a specified number of tasks for a grade.
- Postassessment: evaluation of student performance.

Learning Center

Learning centers can be developed as supplemental instructional aids for enhancing task utilization. The following represent some of these resources:

- Loop films, slides, filmstrips for viewing skills.
- Books, charts, pictures, and worksheets for cognitizing skills.
- VTR for evaluating skill performance.
- Prerecorded tapes (record tasks with tone to signal stop) for helping students with reading disabilities.

Evaluation

Tasks can serve as the diagnostic tool for assessing:

- Entry skill level.
- Continuous performance progress.
- Exit skill level (See Figure 2.4 for one method of recording each pupil's exit level of performance).

One example for maintaining a profile on each pupil's performance is suggested in Figure 2.4. The left hand column lists the number of the tasks for each of the skills in an activity, in this case basketball. A check mark is recorded indicating completion of the task. In the next sections, "Written Work," "Attitudes," and "Game Play," the teacher profiles a percentage score based on both objective and subjective evaluation. The last column is for any general comments and/or observations that the teacher might have. Scale items under "Attitudes" and "Game Play" can be programmed to criteria deemed more appropriate by the teacher. At the end of the unit, the card is filed for various uses. It might serve as a record for grading, conferences with parents, but, perhaps most importantly, it provides a profile for next year's entry level.

TASK CARD				
Student Name: John Doe				
Activity: Badminton				
Grade: 7				
Skill: Serve				

TASK	**Completed Student Check**	**Evaluation**		
		Self	Peer	Teacher
Task #1. In partners A serves ten shuttles against the wall above the line. B checks partner for: • feet stationary on serve and behind line. • racket contact shuttle *below* waist. • racket hand below wrist on contact. Complete eight out of ten. Reverse. If after three trials either is not successful, both report to teacher.				
Task #2. In partners, go to badminton court *without* a net. Legally serve five shuttles from court to opposite diagonal court. Look at chalkboard for boundary diagram. Complete four out of five legal serves. Reverse. If after three trials either is not successful, both report to teacher.				
Task #3. Stay on same court. Serve five shuttles short and five deep so that short fall in front 1/3 of court and deep fall in back 1/3 of court. Complete 3 out of 5 each. Reverse. If after three trials either is not successful, both report to teacher.				
Task #4. Go to court with a net. Repeat Task #3.				
Task #5. In partners A serves five shuttles. B stands on receiving court and tries to return serve (no play.) For each legal serve that is unreturned to A's side (outside boundary lines) score 1 point for A. If legally returned, score one point for B. If A fails to legally serve, no point but loss of trial. Reverse. Total points. List serving strategies.				

Figure 2.1 Task Card Example from Mueller, R. (1976). Task cards. In AAHPER (Ed.), *Personalized learning in physical education.* **Reprinted by permission of the American Alliance for Health, Physical Education, Recreation and Dance, 1900 Association Drive, Reston, Virginia 22091.**

ACTION-ORIENTED TASK CARD
(RECIPROCAL STYLE)

Soccer: Instep kick

Description of the Task: Select a partner you would like to work with during the next learning experience. The two of you get a soccer ball and select one of the wall stations. Decide who is the doer and who will observe first. The doer will place the ball on the designated spot and, taking one step, will kick the ball using the *instep kick*. The observer will watch and make corrections regarding what the doer did well or not well. After each kick the observer will tell the doer what he did correctly and incorrectly. You will also record the accuracy of the kick, but wait until you get your feedback from the observer. Each of you will take 20 repetitions.

Hints to learner and observer — you are to look for:
  (1) Nonkicking foot placed alongside of ball.
  (2) Toe of nonkicking foot pointed toward target.
  (3) Head down until moment of contact.
  (4) Contact with instep (toe pointed down and slightly toward nonkicking foot).

Doer:
  (1) Listen to feedback and try to concentrate on the phase causing you the most difficulty.
  (2) Don't forget to record accuracy (after feedback).
Evaluation feedback: (1) I'll be moving around to assist the observer. If you have any questions, ask the observer first. If he/she can't help, let the observer contact me. (2) Record the target hits (X) per appropriate trial blank.

1	2	3	4	5	6	7	8	9	10

11	12	13	14	15	16	17	18	19	20

Teacher Approval:

Figure 2.2 Task Card Example from Mueller, R. (1976). Task cards. In AAHPER (Ed.), *Personalized learning in physical education.* **Reprinted by permission of the American Alliance for Health, Physical Education, Recreation and Dance, 1900 Association Drive, Reston, Virginia 22091.**

INFORMATION ACTION — ORIENTED TASK CARD
(Individual Program — Teacher Design Style)

Basketball: Jump Shot

Information on the Jump Shot: You are to select one of the following to gain information on the jump shot:

1. live demonstration and explanation.
2. reading about jump shot.
3. silent loop film — analyze the movement. You may trust the movements to memory or write them down. Regardless, after 10 shots and 15 shots, return to the source and review your insights.

Description of the Task: After you attain the information, select a basketball and a basket and choose one of the distance arcs marked on the floor. On this paper mark your selected arc before you start. You will take 20 shots from your selected distance.

Hints to the Learner:
(1) Stay with your selected distance, don't change it; take all 20 shots. (2) If you are having problems, think about the techniques (go back to the source if necessary). (3) Remember that you are responsible for your own self-evaluation. (4) You are to return to the source after the 10th and 15th shots.

Evaluation/Feedback:

Mark by crossing out.

3′	5′	7′	9′	11′	15′	17′	18′	19′	20′

1	2	3	4	5	6	7	8	9	10

11	12	13	14	15	16	17	18	19	20

Your Evaluation Comments:
   What was your result?
   What was your most consistent factor (right-wrong)?
   What did you change?
   Were you more successful or less as a result of your change?
   What changes would you make now if you had 20 more shots?
   Are you ready to move on?

Teacher Approval:

Figure 2.3 Task Card Example from Mueller, R. (1976). Task cards. In AAHPER (Ed.), *Personalized learning in physical education.* **Reprinted by permission of the American Alliance for Health, Physical Education, Recreation and Dance, 1900 Association Drive, Reston, Virginia 22091.**

PERFORMANCE RECORD

STUDENT — Scott Smith   ACTIVITY — Basketball

Tasks (Scott Smith):

Tasks	Pass	Dribble	Goal Setting	Lay-Up	Guarding	Jump
1	×	×	×	×	×	×
2	×	×	×	×	×	×
3	×	×	×	×	×	×
4	×	×	×	×	×	
5	×	×	×	×	×	
6	×	×	×	×		
7	×	×	×	×		
8	×	×		×		
9		×		×		
10		×		×		
11		×				
12		×				
13						
14						
15						
16						

Percent scale: -90-, -80-, -70-, -60-, -50-, -40-, -30-, -20-, -10-, -0-

Written:
- Work Sheets
- Quiz
- Test

Attitudes:
- Dressed
- Busy
- Helpful
- Sports-manship

Game Play:
- Skill
- Position
- Strategy
- Aggressive

Comments:
- good skills
- absent 1 wk medical reasons
- needs to control temper

Figure 2.4

GENERAL ORGANIZING SUGGESTIONS

- The quantitative dimension within the skill tasks is arbitrary and should be modified according to the teacher's perception of student capability.
- The qualitative dimension can be assessed by the teacher, gym leader, group leader, partner, individual student, or any combination of these.
- Since all tasks are written for the right-handed student, teachers must make the necessary adjustments for left-handed students.
- Tasks can be duplicated for student or group use. Additional replications can be made in the form of posters, charts, transparencies, and task cards.
- Safety is essential and must be emphasized in the organizational design of individual and small group work. (See safety guidelines in the following section.)
- Equipment should be utilized so that maximum participation is accomplished. Example: various kinds of balls can be used in the development of ball handling skills.

SAFETY GUIDELINES FOR UTILIZING TASKS

- Stations and apparatus should be spaced for safe traffic patterns.
- The area designated for executing a task should be adequately sized for the number of students involved.
- When establishing an area for executing a task, boundaries should be designated and marked through the use of cones in order to avoid student collisions with those executing different tasks.
- A safe surface and environment should be provided for executing the tasks.
- Equipment should be inspected often for sound construction and signs of wear.
- Spotters should be employed when tasks warrant their use.
- Students should be instructed to wear proper shoes and apparel to avoid falling (slipping) and interference with clothes.
- Students should be instructed not to interfere with others who are executing tasks.
- Students should be taught to compete with themselves, not others, when executing the tasks.
- Students should not be required to execute tasks that are markedly beyond their ability.
- Students should be instructed to keep a clear distance from flying equipment such as bats, shot puts, rackets, etc., when they are used.

APPLICATIONS FOR THE TASK LEARNING EXPERIENCES

We would like to suggest some specific practical applications for utilizing task learning experiences:

- The task learning experiences may be projected through use of transparencies thus allowing the students to read and initiate the tasks on an individual basis.
- The task learning experiences may be recorded on cassettes for the student to hear and then execute. A signal may be used to assist the student in knowing when to turn the tape player off. The use of cassettes is especially appropriate in the lower grades and for those students who have a learning impairment or who experience difficulty with reading.
- The task learning experiences may be used by the students as a means of contracting for an individualized program. The tasks in the text are behaviorally written for simple evaluation.
- The task learning experiences may be placed on task cards or task sheets which can serve as a means of instruction with self-evaluation, reciprocal, or teacher assessment. (See samples in this chapter.)
- The task learning experiences may be used as a challenge to self skill. Tasks of similar skill level may be written on paper and placed in a box for drawing. The student must perform the skill correctly and then exchange papers with another student.
- The task learning experiences may be used by students as an evaluative process with a video-tape recorder. Since the tasks are definitive, the video-tape recorder provides an excellent means for evaluation.
- The task learning experiences may be listed on charts at stations and the students can rotate after completing the tasks at that station. (See types of stations in this chapter.)
- The task learning experiences may be used as student activities during noon recess. The tasks can be posted so they are visible to those on the playground or in the gymnasium.
- The task learning experiences may be utilized during a parents' gym night to demonstrate to the community an overview of the physical education program. The parents can be given sample task cards to execute.
- The task learning experiences may be used by the teacher as behavioral objectives in lesson planning since they are written in measurable terms.
- The task learning experiences may be used by substitute teachers or classroom teachers who are not well informed in the area of physical education content.
- The task learning experience may be used to chart a student's profile of skill acquisition from grade to grade by establishing a progressive record of completed tasks.
- Original task learning experiences may be written by students as an exercise in intellectual creativity and kinesthetic awareness.

- Additional task learning experiences may be written by the teacher for units not included in this text. (See task preparation in this chapter.)

TASK PREPARATION

The preparation of tasks is more time consuming than difficult. The process is simplified by examining the following components of the task model (see figure 2.5) in isolation:

1. Set the task goal. Reduce the overall learning objective to its simplest form.
2. Construct the task. Use movement factors and movement criteria to define the task expectations.
   - 2.1.   Movement Factors:
       - 2.1.1 Body Movement: Locomotor, nonlocomotor, manipulative skills.
       - 2.1.2 Body Part: Head, chest, arms, wrists, legs, feet, etc.
       - 2.1.3 Body Quality: Force, agility, speed, rhythm, endurance, balance, flexibility, flow, accuracy, etc.
   - 2.2   Movement Criteria:
       - 2.2.1 Behavior: What is to be done.
       - 2.2.2 Conditions: How behavior is to be performed.
       - 2.2.3 Standard: Level of performance.
3. State the task as a behavioral objective.
4. Restate the task according to behavioral expectations.
5. Arrange a sequence of tasks (see figure 2.6).

After the task goal has been established and a task is processed into a behavioral expectation, then sequencing follows. The development of a range of tasks proceeds from simple to complex. Skill performance begins at the lowest level with the least internal and external interference and graduates to a simulated game that provides game elements. The final level of performance resides within the complexities of a game construct which is heightened by stress factors.

Mosston (1966) calls for tasks written either quantitatively or qualitatively. Quantitative tasks are measurable in terms of repetitions, duration, successful completions, etc., whereas qualitative tasks require judgment on the quality of performance. Form, which has an aesthetic value, is most frequently applied to qualitative tasks.

Mueller (1976) suggests that tasks be written either as action-oriented or information/action. Briefly defined, action-oriented tasks require the learner to practice some movement which has been taught or some knowledge that has been previously processed.

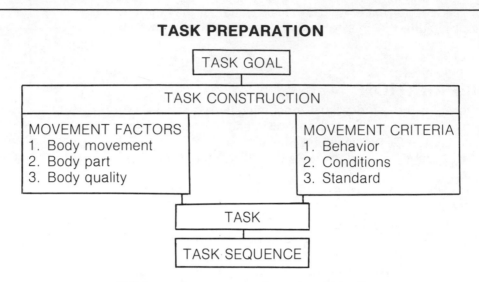

TASK PREPARATION

TASK GOAL

TASK CONSTRUCTION

MOVEMENT FACTORS
1. Body movement
2. Body part
3. Body quality

MOVEMENT CRITERIA
1. Behavior
2. Conditions
3. Standard

TASK

TASK SEQUENCE

TASK PREPARATION EXAMPLE

Task Goal: Striking an object with the foot

Task Construction:
    Movement factors:
1. Body movement   — kicking
2. Body part   — foot
3. Body quality   — strength
    Movement criteria:
1. Behavior   — student will kick
2. Conditions   — from punt position
3. Standard   — for distance

Task stated as a behavioral objective: The student will kick a
    football from a punt position for distance and measure the longest
    of three trials.

Task restated: In partners, A will punt a football three times for dis-
    tance, B marks and retrieves. A and B measure the best distance.
    Record and reverse.

Sequence: Write tasks to include the following information.
    1. Review loops, charts, and film strips on punting.
    2. Punt without a ball and concentrate on form and mechanics.
    3. Punt using a ball.
    4. Add height — might set some problems.
    5. Add distance.
    6. Add accuracy.
    7. Add the punt from a center hike.
    8. Add a defensive player.
    9. Add more defensive players to simulate a game.

Figure 2.5

TASK LEVELING (SEQUENCING)		
LESS DIFFICULT	TASK	MORE DIFFICULT
	Using a full swing serve the tennis ball two out of five times into a legal court from the proper area behind the baseline.	
	From a distance of fifteen feet, knock down the Indian club by kicking the ball.	
	Bunt five pitched balls so that each travels about 20 feet.	

Can you suggest some tasks that are less difficult? More difficult?

Figure 2.6.

Information/action tasks obligate the learner to obtain the subject matter information necessary for movement practice (figures 2.2 and 2.3).

Rink (1981) proposes that tasks be designed that foster refining, extending, and applying relationships. A refining sequence of tasks leads the learner toward a higher quality level of a particular movement or movement pattern. Extending the task increases the difficulty by integrating more movements or changing the movement environment, and applying tasks focuses on using the newly acquired knowledge or skill in a particular movement setting.

THREE

Supervised Task Programming: A Strategy for Individualizing

THE WHAT OF INDIVIDUALIZING

Individualized learning encourages each student to proceed through a unit of instruction according to his/her own personal inventory of abilities, needs, and interests. A major goal of individualization is to promote self-directed learners who are capable of engaging effectively in the process of decision making. This goal is complicated by the fact that individual students vary widely in their readiness to function as independent learners. However, proponents of individualized education suggest that to retain a formal school setting where there is only one set of learning expectations for all students, where a single standard of measurement prevails, where instruction proceeds at a fixed-exposure rate, where only one learning style is recognized, and where the whole teaching-learning process is bound together by group norms is to disclaim the very ideal of American education which purports to teach groups of individuals.

If one is serious about individualizing instruction, then one must consider *what* is to be learned. What does the student already know, what does the student want to know, and what does the student need to know? Then one must look at content analysis. What should be the total amount of content presented, in what sequence should the content be presented, what should be the size of the steps in the sequences, at what rate should it be presented, and what should be the mode of presentation? Another consideration is the *how* of learning. How is the student motivated to learn, how does the student learn most effectively, how will the teaching agents of teacher, peer, and materials best accommodate learning, and how will learning be assessed? Still another consideration is the *degree* or amounts of exposure necessary for optimal learning. How much should be learned, how much time does the student need, how much teacher supervision is needed, how much evaluative and supportive feedback is needed, how much variation in the learning task is needed, and how much social interaction is needed?

At first glance one might argue that the above are all common planning procedures used by good teachers. True, but the difference lies in the fact that the focus of teacher planning is on individual students who comprise the class and not on the class comprised of individual students.

INDIVIDUALIZED EDUCATION APPROACHES

Individualized education requires the learner to take responsibility for attaining a level of proficiency for his/her performance. This can occur in a variety of settings. Variations of individualized programming provide a spectrum of loosely to tightly knit approaches. At one end are those programs which allow the student to select from a list of offerings and at some level of difficulty. Swimming would be a good example, where one has a choice ranging from beginning swimming to water safety instructor. However, once the student enters such a class, usually group-regulated instruction prevails. Another approach provides all students with a core of information which is delivered *en masse* followed by optional activity choices for the rest of the unit. An example might be a six week tennis unit where the main skills and game play techniques are covered in group instruction during the first three weeks. For the remainder, students may choose tournament play, continue to practice skills and game play, complete so many games at a near-by racquet club or public courts, watch and report on school, university, or televised competition, write a research paper on the same aspect of tennis, read and report on the biographies of tennis personalities, and the list could go on.

Another method provides individualized learning opportunities through independent study. Students are excused from regular class and allowed to complete a unit of study and participate in an activity or at a level not offered in the school curriculum. The study plan would include a reporting system, evaluative criteria, and instructor approval. Activity examples might include riflery, scuba diving, ballet, hang gliding, water surfing, etc. These latter two plans usually occur at the senior high or college level.

Contracting or performance agreement offers still another variation in individualized education. The contract is a written agreement between the student and teacher, the contents of which usually specify a description of performance expectations, grading standards, and terms or length of contract. Contracts can range from simple statements to highly structured forms of agreement and may be written to cover a single day to a whole unit of activity.

Unlike the approaches previously described, our final model operationalizes the many features of individualized learning. Such a program allows each pupil to move at his/her pace through a learning unit tailored to meet his/her abilities. The program provides for differences in entry skill level, differences in rate of learning for achieving objectives, and differences in learning outcomes. Essentially, this model gives precise information to the pupil. Learning objectives and experiences are written in behavioral terms, providing description and direction, sequenced learning, and a standard of measurement. Instructional materials and media are available and complement the program package. Pretests and post-tests usually accompany this approach as well as checkpoints throughout the unit. The teacher's role is one of facilitator who works individually with each student.

One can infer from these descriptions that individualized education has several meanings and not necessarily the same meaning for everyone.

SUPERVISED TASK PROGRAMMING

We briefly described teaching methods commonly associated with physical education instruction. We intended that the reader should be aware of different teaching styles and that task learning experiences could be incorporated into any preferred style of teaching. With that in mind, our ambition was threefold: First, that the reader would benefit from a review of methods by gaining a better understanding of the working relationships, weaknesses, and strengths of each method. Second, that one's teaching behavior might be strengthened and/or modified by assimilating some of the aforementioned understanding. And finally, that the teacher would be motivated to consciously apply task programming as a teaching-learning behavior.

While we have shown that all pedagogical strategies can accommodate task application, our intention now is to express our preference, rationalize its significance, and present a model of task strategy.

We believe that task programming, as it relates to both a teaching and learning strategy, supports the fundamental tenets of product learning; and furthermore, we favor a teaching model that includes some of the concepts and components of product learning. While we are not championing a rigorous system of individualized instruction, we are suggesting a paradigm that promotes an interaction of selected precepts and operational elements from individualization as well as other teaching modes. We will refer to this model as Supervised Task Programming. You will note that the word "supervised" appears first, and as such, signals a teacher-centered or teacher-directed intent.

As with any method, each teacher's application varies with inter-pretation and use. However, the following features that comprise

Supervised Task Programming should prevail if maximum learning benefits are to be derived.

SUPERVISED TASK PROGRAMMING

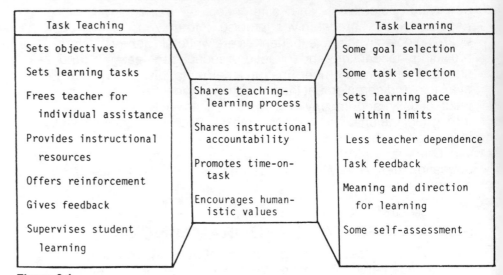

Task Teaching		Task Learning
Sets objectives		Some goal selection
Sets learning tasks		Some task selection
Frees teacher for individual assistance	Shares teaching-learning process	Sets learning pace within limits
Provides instructional resources	Shares instructional accountability	Less teacher dependence
Offers reinforcement	Promotes time-on-task	Task feedback
Gives feedback	Encourages humanistic values	Meaning and direction for learning
Supervises student learning		Some self-assessment

Figure 3.1

1. *Delineation of learning outcomes.* Every teacher should determine at the onset of a unit or course of study what he/she hopes his/her students will know, do, and feel at the completion of the course. This should be translated into performance objectives which serve as a guide for selecting task learning experiences. Linked with setting performance objectives is the learning principle that learning is facilitated when the learner has a clearly established goal in mind.

2. *Provision for different learning rates.* Task programming should allow for individual pacing. The presentation of task learning experiences ought to be flexible enough so that the learner can progress at his/her own rate within the constraints of the course schedule. The use of task cards can aid in self-pacing. A task card might list one or several tasks. In either case, the student completes a task before progressing to the next. Over a given time period students will, and should, vary in the number of completed tasks. Inherent within this system is recognized that the quality of task performance is stressed rather than simply a checklist of completions.

3. *Arrangement of sequential, mastery level tasks.* In the preceding chapter a detailed procedure for writing tasks was described. Learning tasks are derived from course content objectives and provide the pupil with a concise description of what to do, how to do it, and how to measure it. Tasks are written

in mastery terms (that is successful accomplishment before proceeding to the next), and they are sequenced for refinement, extension, and application. Before commencing activity, the student is not only presented with what is expected but how well. The use of learning tasks is undergirded with motor learning principles of which some were noted earlier. Namely, these are:

3.1 Learning is more meaningful when it can be linked with application.

3.2 Learning is more effective when the learner has a clearly established goal in mind.

3.3 Learning should proceed from the simple to complex.

3.4 Self-analysis of skill performance increases the learner's awareness about what constitutes a good performance.

4. *Use of frequent and meaningful feedback.* Feedback should be brief, task-relevant, and often if learning is to be optimally facilitated. Under an instructional plan that employs task learning experiences, immediate feedback is frequently built into the task as mastery criteria. There remains little guesswork about a performance when a target is hit, a pass completed, or a distance achieved. Where measurable outcomes are less explicit, the use of peer observers can help. The teacher can also provide a final checkpoint; however, the amount of teacher input is proportional to teacher need for assessment control. If the student performance fails to meet the preset competency standards, then the student would return to the activity area and continues to work toward mastery. During the "looping effect" some encouragement should be given to the student. The completion of a task can become a reinforcer for attempting another task or a more difficult one.

5. *Advocacy of person-to-person relationships.* Task programming caters to an atmosphere that fosters social transactions in an open communication environment. Student-to-student relationships are promoted through the cooperative sharing of space and equipment, through the reciprocal arrangement of task assessment, and through partner and small grouping formations necessary for task achievement. Teacher-to-students and student-to-teacher interactions. become commonplace as the role of both teacher and student function in a mini-social setting. Teacher behaviors, e.g., observations, encouragement, prescriptions, corrections, reinforcement, assessments, etc., are communicated as face-to-face conversation. Herein lies the opportunity for personalizing or humanizing the educational process.

6. *Presentation of master lessons.* While self-instructive materials are a major learning source of this model, they do not discount the need for whole class presentations. Few would deny that the expected role of the teacher includes conventional methods of whole group instruction. This does not imply that master lessons

need to be lengthy, frequent, or necessarily preliminary to the onset of new content. Instead, the focus should be on deliberate planning that attends to clarity of goals, content relevance, step-by-step explanations, and overall presentation effectiveness — all of which should move the learner toward improved task achievement.

Supervised Task Programming is a teaching-learning strategy that promotes engaging the learner in meaningful interactions with criterion materials and maximum on-task behavior. In summary, Supervised Task Programming relies upon specific learning goals, small units of learning tasks, mastery achievement, flexible learning time, knowledge of results and diagnostic feedback, alternative modes of instruction, and cooperative learning with peers. The schematic model in Figure 3.1 highlights the teaching-learning roles and behaviors that form the primary features of Supervised Task Programming.

FOUR

Application Models for Task Learning Experiences

This chapter presents two different models of how learning experiences may be used to individualize instruction. We offer these two examples recognizing that there are several approaches to individualization but that each school has its own unique set of circumstances which can rationalize its approach. The first model shows how learning experiences can be organized into mini-units and is programmed for upper elementary school students. The second model provides an individualized badminton unit for high school students stressing Supervised Task Programming.

THE USE OF TASK CARDS IN MINI-UNITS OF INSTRUCTION

In the process of utilizing task learning experiences, the teacher can develop the materials into mini-units of instruction. This can be accomplished by selecting tasks according to the student's level of skill acquisition and thus developing appropriate task cards. The mini-units concentrate on one activity for several class sessions moving rapidly from one skill to another. The value of mini-units is that they offer a greater variety of activities that the student can experience and allow the student to work at varying levels of ability within the activity. The units also provide opportunity for students to progress through diverse skills within the activity.

In order to accommodate individual levels of ability, it is suggested that the cards be labeled as beginner, intermediate, or advanced levels and likewise be color coded as to their levels (yellow, red, and blue respectively). These color coded cards could be placed in a permanent file system and even be laminated for extended use. The teacher could define procedures for using and replacing the cards properly. If labeling (beginning, intermediate, and advanced levels) creates peer problems then the colors could be used exclusively.

A feature of individualized instruction that can be utilized with the cards is to place a directive at the bottom of each card indicating the next skill and level to which to progress. This would approximate a type of programmed learning. An example set forth at the bottom of a task card for beginner (yellow) level soccer kick-pass might state "When you have successfully completed all four tasks, move to Beginner (yellow) Level - Kick-Pass." This would allow for diverse levels of student abilities and permit the student to excel or repeat the tasks if necessary. If the teacher desired an evaluation other than the student's self-evaluation, a system could be utilized as the authors have designed in figure 2.1. Another alternative to evaluation would be to have a check-off sheet posted on a wall for the students to mark when they successfully complete a specified task card.

Additional task cards could be constructed to provide culminating activities for the skill acquisition cards. These could be used as a reward when students achieve a certain level of skill. An example of this might be to have students completing the yellow level of skill development in volleyball to join together to play a modified or lead-up game such as "One Bounce Volleyball" or "Keep It Up." The criteria for playing this game might be that when at least eight students have completed or checked off the entire yellow level they may form two teams to play. The culminating activity would exemplify the skill level of the tasks just executed. If there were not an adequate number of students ready to be part of the culminating activity, the task card would give a directive to move to an alternative skill until enough students were available to participate in the culminating activity.

On the following pages several mini-units are presented for teacher use. The mini-units selected and developed are: volleyball, gymnastics, and soccer. For each mini-unit an example of a culminating activity task card has been provided for each level of skill (beginner, intermediate, and advanced). This activity can be adapted for the specific class needs or changed to a more familiar one. It should be noted that it may be necessary to demonstrate or explain the skill analysis to the students prior to executing some of the task cards. After each task in the mini-units, the corresponding task number from the text is placed in parentheses.

VOLLEYBALL MINI-UNIT

Note: A colorful playball can be substituted for a beachball and in some instances may be preferable.

Activity: Volleyball   Skill: Chest Pass
Equipment: Beachball   Level: Beginner
                                          (yellow)

Tasks:
1. Throw a beachball into the air and use a chest pass to send the ball toward a wall. Chest pass the rebounds. (3)
2. Repeat Task # 1 executing as many chest passes as possible in a 30-second time period. (4)
3. In partners, repeat Task #1 sending to a partner instead of a wall. Reverse and repeat. (5)
   When you have successfully completed all three tasks, move to Beginner (yellow) Level — Underhand Serve.

Activity: Volleyball   Skill: Underhand Serve
Equipment: Beachball, 6-foot   Level: Beginner
               line on wall   (yellow)

Tasks:
1. Serve a beachball aiming above a 6-foot line on a wall. (3)
2. Repeat Task #1 contacting the ball on different surfaces. Adjust the ball holding hand at various heights. What happens to the flight pattern? (4)
3. In partners, A serves a beachball to B who is approximately 20 feet away. (5)
   When you have successfully completed all three tasks, move to Beginner (yellow) Level — Overhand Serve.

Activity: Volleyball

Skill: Overhand Serve

Equipment: Beachball, 6-foot and 9-foot line on wall

Level: Beginner (yellow)

Tasks:
1. Take a forward-backward stride position about ten feet from a wall. Toss the beachball into the air and contact the ball with heel of the hand. Repeat five times. (3)
2. Repeat Task #1 aiming above a 6-foot line on the wall. (4)
3. Repeat Task #1 aiming between the 6-foot line and the 9-foot line on the wall. Complete 10 serves between the lines. (5)

When you have successfully completed all three tasks, move to Beginner (yellow) Level — Dig Pass.

Activity: Volleyball

Skill: Dig Pass

Equipment: Balloon, Beachball

Level: Beginner (yellow)

Tasks:
1. Use a balloon and execute the dig pass whenever it falls to waist level. (2)
2. In partners, A hits a dig pass with the balloon to B. B returns the balloon to A with a dig pass. (3)
3. Repeat Tasks #1 and #2 using a beachball. (4)

When you have successfully completed all three tasks, move to Beginner (yellow) Level — Culminating Activity OR to Intermediate (red) Level — Chest Pass.

Activity: Volleyball   Skill: Culminating
Equipment: Beachball, Net   Level: Beginner
                                                       (yellow)

Play the game "One-Bounce Volleyball" as described by Blake and
Volp (1964, p. 166). This game is played similar to volleyball except
each time the ball crosses the net it must bounce once (but not more
than once) before it is returned. The server has two tries to serve
successfully. No player can hit the ball more than once before
another player hits it, but any number of players can hit the ball to get
it over the net.

When you have played "One-Bounce Volleyball" for 15 minutes,
move to Intermediate (red) Level — Chest Pass.

Activity: Volleyball   Skill: Chest Pass
Equipment: Beachball, Rope   Level: Intermediate
                    Extended at 10 ft.   (red)

Tasks:
1. In partners, execute 10 chest passes volleying a beachball from a
   distance of 10 feet. Increase the distance to 15 feet. Increase to 20
   feet. (6)
2. In groups of five, A tosses the beachball up and executes a chest
   pass to any of the four students grouped in a circle. The receiver
   uses a chest pass to send the ball to another, etc. Attempt to keep
   the ball in play as long as possible. (7)
3. In partners, A tosses the beachball into air and uses the chest pass
   to send the ball to B over a 10-foot rope extended horizontally
   across the gymnasium. (9)

When you have successfully completed all three tasks, move to
Intermediate (red) Level — Underhand Serve.

Activity: Volleyball

Equipment: Beachball,
                  Volleyball, Net

Skill: Underhand
           Serve

Level: Intermediate
           (red)

Tasks

1. Serve a beachball over the net into the opposite court from a point halfway between the serving line and net. (7)
2. Make a volleyball court as diagrammed.

X ➡	10	20	30

   Serve the beachball five times attempting to make the ball land in the high scoring zone. Stand halfway between serving line and net. (8)
3. Repeat Tasks #1 and #2 using a volleyball. (9)

When you have successfully completed all three tasks, move to Intermediate (red) Level — Overhand Serve.

Activity: Volleyball

Equipment: Beachball,
                  Volleyball, Net

Skill: Overhand
           Serve

Level: Intermediate
           (red)

Tasks:

1. In partners, using the overhand serve, A serves the beachball to B who is 30 feet away. Try to maintain a horizontal flight. Reverse and repeat five times. (6)
2. In partners, standing at opposite midcourts, A and B execute the overhand serve back and forth with a beachball. (7)
3. Repeat task #2 standing behind the serving line near the center of the court. (8)
4. Repeat Tasks #1-3 using a volleyball. (9)

When you have successfully completed all four tasks, move to Intermediate (red) Level — Set Pass.

Activity: Volleyball
Equipment: 2 Beachballs,
              Rope at 10 ft.

Skill: Set Pass
Level: Intermediate
         (red)

Tasks:
1. In groups of six, circle set pass — Players set pass the beachball to anyone in the circle as many times as possible without allowing the ball to hit the floor. Continue for five minutes. (10)
2. Repeat Task #1 adding a second ball to the circle set pass. (11)
3. In partners, A set passes the beachball to B over a 10 foot rope extended horizontally across gymnasium. Continue back and forth for five minutes. (12)

When you have successfully completed all three tasks, move to the Intermediate (red) Level — Spike.

Activity: Volleyball
Equipment: Beachball, Net,
              Chair

Skill: Spike
Level: Intermediate
         (red)

Tasks:
1. Stand beside the net, jump, turn body, and extend the arm closest to the net imitating a downward hit. Repeat five times. (4)
2. Stand next to the net, toss a beachball into the air, jump, and spike it. Repeat five times. (5)
3. In partners, A holds a beachball just above the net by standing on a chair and allows B to improve timing by jumping and spiking it. Repeat five times. Reverse. (6)

When you have successfully completed all three tasks, move to Intermediate (red) Level — Block.

Activity: Volleyball   Skill: Block
Equipment: Beachball, Net,   Level: Intermediate
           Chair   (red)

Tasks:
1. In partners, A stands opposite B (across net). A jumps up imitating a spike while B jumps to imitate a block. Practice five times to improve blocking reaction time. Reverse. (6)
2. Toss a beachball high against the wall, jump, and block the rebound. Repeat 10 times. (7)
3. In partners, A throws a beachball forcefully across the top of the net by standing on a chair. B must block the beachball. Repeat five times. Reverse. (8)

When you have successfully completed all three tasks, move to Intermediate (red) Level — Dig Pass.

Activity: Volleyball   Skill: Dig Pass
Equipment: Beachball, Net,   Level: Intermediate
           Chair   (red)

Tasks:
1. In partners, A tosses a beachball high into the air and B dig passes. After five dig passes, reverse. (5)
2. Use a beachball and execute the dig pass against a wall 10 times. (6)
3. In partners, A stands on a chair across the net and throws the beachball downward to B who is prepared to execute a dig pass. Repeat five times. Reverse. (7)

When you have successfully completed all three tasks, move to Intermediate (red) Level — Culminating activity OR to Advanced (blue) Level — Chest Pass.

Activity: Volleyball   Skill: Culminating
                                           Activity
Equipment: Beachball, Net   Level: Intermediate
                                           (red)

Play a game of "Beachball Volleyball" using all the rules and skills of volleyball. The only variation is the use of a beachball or playball.

When you have played "Beachball Volleyball" for 15 minutes, move to Advanced (blue) Level — Chest Pass.

Activity: Volleyball   Skill: Chest Pass
Equipment: Volleyball, Net   Level: Advanced
                                           (blue)

Tasks:
1. In groups of three, A tosses the volleyball to self and executes a chest pass to B. B set passes to C. Rotate and repeat five times.
2. In groups of four, A tosses the volleyball to self and executes a chest pass to B. B set passes to C. C spikes the volleyball over the net to D who retrieves the ball. Rotate and repeat 10 times. (10)
3. Repeat Task #2 with D attempting to block the spiked ball. (11)

When you have successfully completed all three tasks, move to Advanced (blue) Level — Underhand Serve.

Activity: Volleyball   Skill: Underhand
                                           Serve
Equipment: Volleyball, Net   Level: Advanced
                                           (blue)

Tasks:
1. Serve a volleyball using an underhand serve to the right back position. Complete one out of five, 3/5, 4/5. (11)
2. Repeat Task #1 serving to the left back position. (12)
3. Repeat Task #1 serving to the right forward position. (13)
4. Repeat Task #1 serving to the left forward position. (14)

When you have successfuly completed all four tasks, move to Advanced (blue) Level — Overhand Serve.

Activity: Volleyball   Skill: Overhand
                                                      Serve
Equipment: Volleyball, Net   Level: Advanced
                                                      (blue)

Tasks:
1. Serve a volleyball using an overhand serve to serve to the right back position. Complete one out of five, 3/5, 4/5. (11)
2. Repeat Task #1 serving to the center back position. (11)
3. Repeat Task #1 serving to the left back position. (11)
4. Repeat Task #1 serving to the right forward position. (11)
5. Repeat Task #1 serving to the left forward position. (11)

When you have successfully completed all five tasks, move to Advanced (blue) Level — Set Pass.

Activity: Volleyball   Skill: Set Pass
Equipment: Volleyball, Net   Level: Advanced
                                                      (blue)

Tasks:
1. In groups of three, A chest passes to B; B set passes to C; C spikes the volleyball. Rotate and repeat five times. (14)
2. Repeat Task #1 using a net. (15)
3. Repeat Task #1 using a backward set pass by tilting the head back and arching the body. (17)

When you have successfully completed all three tasks, move to Advanced (blue) Level — Spike.

Activity: Volleyball   Skill: Spike
Equipment: Volleyball, Net   Level: Advanced
            Chair   (blue)

Tasks:
1. Stand next to the net, toss a volleyball into the air, jump, and spike it. Repeat five times. (5)
2. In partners, A holds a volleyball just above the net by standing on a chair and allows B to improve timing by jumping and spiking it, Repeat five times. Reverse. (6)
3. In groups of three, A stands to the side and tosses a volleyball high to B who is close to the net for the spike. C retrieves the spike. Rotate positions and repeat five times. (7)

When you have successfully completed all three tasks, move to Advanced (blue) Level — Block.

Activity: Volleyball   Skill: Block
Equipment: Volleyball, Net,   Level: Advanced
            Chair   (blue)

Tasks:
1. Toss a volleyball high against the wall, jump, and block the rebound. Repeat five times. (7)
2. In partners, A throws a volleyball forcefully across the top of the net by standing on a chair. B must block the volleyball. Repeat five times. Reverse. (8)
3. In groups of three, A stands to the side and tosses a volleyball to B who is close to the net in order to spike. C blocks the spike. Rotate positions and repeat five times. (9)

When you have successfully completed all three tasks, move to advanced (blue) Level — Dig Pass.

Activity: Volleyball   Skill: Dig Pass
Equipment: Volleyball, Net,   Level: Advanced
              Chair   (blue)

Tasks:
1. In partners, A stands on a chair across the net and throws the
    volleyball downward to B who is prepared to execute a dig pass.
    Repeat five times. Reverse. (7)
2. In groups of three, A throws the volleyball to B at waist height who
    then uses a dig pass to send the ball over the net to the back court
    to C who retrieves the ball and rolls it back. Rotate positions and
    repeat five times. (9)
3. Repeat Task #2, A volleying the ball to B instead of throwing.
    (10)

When you have successfully completed all three tasks, move to
Advanced (blue) Level — Culminating Activity.

Activity: Volleyball   Skill: Culminating
                                                          Activity
Equipment: Volleyball, Net   Level: Advanced
                                                          (blue)

Play a volleyball game.
Continue play for a set time period.

GYMNASTICS MINI-UNIT

Note: Equipment stations should be set up in advance to allow smooth transition from one skill to another.

Activity: Gymnastics   Skill: Balance Beam
Equipment: Balance Beam   Level: Beginner
                                           (yellow)

Tasks:
1. Walk forward across the beam. Repeat three times. (1)
2. Walk backward across the beam. Repeat three times. (2)
3. Walk forward dipping the foot below the side of the beam and then up. Repeat three times. (4)
4. Walk halfway across the beam and pivot turn on the toes (180° — 1/2 turn). Repeat twice. (9)

When you have successfully completed all four tasks, move to Beginner (yellow) Level — Side Horse Vaulting OR Beginner (yellow) Level — Balance Beam Culminating Activity.

Activity: Gymnastics   Skill: Side Horse
                                           Vaulting
Equipment: Side Horse,   Level: Beginner
             Reuther Board   (yellow)

Tasks:
1. Take a short run toward the horse and practice the hurdle or jump on the reuther board. Just the hands contact the horse while the feet return to the board without executing any type of vault. Repeat 10 times. (1)
2. Squat-On Vault — Take a run, jump onto the board, land on the horse with both feet together inside the hands (squat position), stand up, and jump off. Repeat five times. (5)
3. Repeat Task #3 jumping off the horse with the legs in a straddle position. (6)
4. Repeat Task #3 turning in the air while jumping off the horse. Try a 1/4, 1/2, or full turn in the air. (7)

When you have successfully completed all four tasks, move to Beginner (yellow) Level — Uneven Bars OR to Beginner (yellow) Level — Uneven Bars OR to Beginner (yellow) Level — Side Horse Culminating Activity.

Activity: Gymnastics   Skill: Uneven Bars
Equipment: Uneven Bars   Level: Beginner
                                                     (yellow)

Tasks:
1. Front Support Mount — Jump up and grasp (overgrip) the low bar and rest (balance) the thighs on the bar while keeping the head and shoulders forward. Hold for six seconds. Repeat three times. (1)
2. Swan Balance — Execute a front support and release the grip (bring the arms overhead) and balance on the thighs. Hold for three seconds. Repeat three times. (4)
3. Push Away — Execute a front support and throw the legs backward away from the bar. The legs then return to the front support position on the bar. Push away three times. Repeat three times. (6)
4. Quarter Turn Dismount —From a stride position on the low bar, lift the back leg sideways and up over the bar executing a 1/4 turn and landing on the mat. Repeat five times. (13)

When you have successfully completed all four tasks, move to Beginner (yellow) Level — Parallel Bars OR to Beginner (yellow) Level — Uneven Bars Culminating Activity.

Activity: Gymnastics   Skill: Parallel Bars
Equipment: Parallel Bars   Level: Beginner
                                                     (yellow)

Tasks:
1. Hand Walk — While in a straight arm support, take "steps" forward with the hands (shift body weight from one hand to the other). Hand walk the length of the bars. Repeat twice. (2)
2. Repeat Task #1 "walking" backward. (3)
3. Front Hook — While in a straight arm support (straight arms support the body with the elbows locked), swing legs forward and up resting the feet on the bars. Straighten the body then release the legs for the dismount. Repeat five times. (4)
4. Rear Hook — Repeat Task #3 swinging the legs backward and up. (5)

When you have successfully completed all four tasks, move to Beginner (yellow) Level — Low Horizontal Bar OR Beginner (yellow) Level — Parallel Bars Culminating Activity.

Activity: Gymnastics   Skill: Low
                                              Horizontal Bar
Equipment: Low Horizontal Bar   Level: Beginner
                                              (yellow)

Tasks:
1. Flexed Arm Hang — Grasp the bar (overgrip) and hang with the
    arms in a bent elbow position. Hold for six seconds. Repeat three
    times. (2)
2. Front Swing — Execute a flexed arm hang and swing the legs
    forward from the hips keeping the body straight. Swing four times.
    Repeat three times. (3)
3. Pike Position Hang — Execute a flexed arm hang and bring
    straight legs up so they extend at right angles to the body with the
    toes pointed. Hold for three seconds. Repeat three times. (9)
4. Front Hand Support — Grasp the bar (overgrip) and pull the body
    up so the hips rest and balance on the bar. Hold for 10 seconds.
    Repeat four times. (11)

When you have successfully completed all four tasks, move to
Beginner (yellow) Level — Still rings OR Beginner (yellow) Level —
Low Horizontal Bar Culminating Activity.

Activity: Gymnastics   Skill: Still Rings
Equipment: Set of Rings   Level: Beginner
                                              (yellow)

Tasks:
1. Extended Arm Hang — Grasp the rings and hang with straight
    arms. Hold for six seconds. Repeat three times. (1)
2. Flexed Arm Hang — Grasp the rings and hang with the arms in a
    bent elbow position. Hold for six seconds. Repeat three times. (2)
3. Tuck Position (knee lift) — Execute a flexed arm hang and raise
    bent knees toward the chest. Hold for three seconds. Repeat
    three times. (3)

When you have successfully completed all three tasks, move to
Intermediate (red) Level — Balance Beam OR Beginner (yellow)
Level — Still Ring Culminating Activity.

Activity: Gymnastics   Skill: Balance Beam
Equipment: Balance Beam   Level: Intermediate
                                                (red)

Tasks:
1. Front Lean Mount — Lean on the side of the beam and support
    the body. Swing one leg over to a straddle position. Hold three
    seconds. Repeat four times. (20)
2. Balance on hands and knees on the beam raising a leg upward
    and backward (knee scale). Hold balance three seconds. Repeat
    three times. (14)
3. Balance on the beam in a stork stand. (Balance on one leg with
    other leg bent so the foot rests on the knee). Hold balance three
    seconds. Repeat four times. (15)
4. Jump Half Turn Dismount — Jump off the end of the beam turning
    the body 180° before landing. Repeat four times. (23)

When you have successfully completed all four tasks, move to
Intermediate (red) Level—Side Horse Vaulting OR Intermediate (red)
Level—Balance Beam Culminating Activity.

Activity: Gymnastics   Skill: Side Horse
                                                Vaulting
Equipment: Side Horse,   Level: Intermediate
              Reuther Board   (red)

Tasks:
1. Straddle-On Vault — Take a run, jump onto the board, land on the
    horse with the legs spread apart outside the hands (straddle
    position). Push off with the hands and land with the feet together
    on the floor. Repeat four times. (9)
2. Wolf-On Vault — Take a run, jump onto the board, bring one leg
    up to the horse in a squat position with the other leg extended
    straight out to the side. Pause then jump to land. Repeat three
    times. (10)
3. Flank Vault — Take a run, jump onto the board, legs extend to one
    side and swing over the horse (weight on one hand only). The
    side of the body is parallel to the horse. Repeat three times. (11)

When you have successfully completed all three tasks, move to
Intermediate (red) Level — Uneven Bars OR Intermediate (red) Level
— Side Horse Vaulting Culminating Activity.

Activity: Gymnastics   Skill: Uneven Bars
Equipment: Uneven Bars   Level: Intermediate
                                             (red)

Tasks:
1. Pull Over to Front Support Mount — Grasp the low bar (overgrip) and swing the legs upward and around the bar to a front support. The upper torso should drop back as the arms flex (bend) to pull the body around. Hold for six seconds. Repeat three times. (2)
2. Shoot Through — Execute a push-away and as the legs are thrown backward bring one leg upward and forward over the bar ending in a stride position. Hold for three seconds. Repeat three times. (7)
3. Back Hip Circle — Execute a front support. Push away from the bar and as the hips touch the bar, throw the legs forward and upward rotating around the bar. Adjust the grip of the hands and return to a front support. Repeat four times. (8)
4. Swing Under Dismount — From a front support on the low bar, lower the body behind the bar while raising the legs upward. Once the torso is under the bar, extend the legs upward, forward, and then outward followed by a release of the bar with the hands. Land with the arms extended overhead. Repeat five times. (14)

When you have successfully completed all four tasks, move to Intermediate (red) Level — Parallel Bars OR Intermediate (red) Level — Uneven Bars Culminating Activity.

Activity: Gymnastics   Skill: Parallel Bars
Equipment: Parallel Bars   Level: Intermediate (red)

Tasks:
1. Straight Arm Support Mount — Jump or have a spotter lift the student to the straight arm support position. (Straight arms support body with elbows locked). Hold three seconds. Repeat four times. (15)
2. Straddle Seat — While in a straight arm support, swing the legs forward and over the bars into a straddle position. Balance on the upper thighs. Balance for three seconds. Push the body up with the arms and swing the legs down, then dismount. Repeat three times. (7)
3. Straddle Travel — Repeat Task #2 eliminating the dismount. Swing the legs down and up to a new straddle position. Travel the length of the bars, then dismount. Repeat twice. (8).
4. Inverted Hang—While holding the bars, pull into a tucked upside down position. Extend the legs and hang. Hang for three seconds. Dismount by tucking the body and returning to a stand. Repeat three times. (9)
5. Rear Vault Dismount—From a straight arm support, swing both legs forward over the right bar. Simultaneously hold the right bar with the left hand and release the right hand. Land beside the bars. Repeat four times. (17)

When you have successfully completed all five tasks, move to Intermediate (red) Level—Low Horizontal Bar OR Intermediate (red) Level—Parallel Bars Culminating Activity.

Activity: Gymnastics   Skill: Low Horizontal
                                            Bar
Equipment: Low Horizontal Bar   Level: Intermediate
                                            (red)

Tasks:
1. Knee Hang—Grasp the bar (overgrip) and bring both legs up through the bar. Release the hands and hang from the back of the bent knees. Dismount by regrasping the bar. Hold for eight seconds. Repeat twice. (12)
2. One Knee Hang—Repeat Task #1 with the hooking of only one knee over the bar. (14)
3. One Knee Mount—Execute a one knee hang. Extend the free leg backward bringing the hips toward the bar while extending the arms. Pull up to a side stride position on the bar with the one knee on the bar and the other knee extended. Hold eight seconds. Repeat three times. (15)

When you have successfully completed all three tasks, move to Intermediate (red) Level—Still Rings OR Intermediate (red) Level—Low Horizontal Bar Culminating Activity.

Activity: Gymnastics   Skill: Still Rings
Equipment: Set of Rings   Level: Intermediate
                                            (red)

Tasks:
1. Pike Position—Execute a flexed arm hang and bring straight legs up so they extend at right angles to the body (horizontal) with the toes pointed. Hold for three seconds. Repeat twice. (4)
2. Bicycle—Execute a flexed arm hang and move knees as if riding a bicycle. Repeat three times, each time bicycling for six seconds. (6)
3. Pull-ups—Raise and lower the body while grasping the rings thus alternating between a flexed and extended arm hang. The chin should touch the hands each time. Do five pull-ups. Repeat twice. (7)

When you have successfully completed all three tasks, move to Advanced (blue) Level—Balance Beam OR Intermediate (red) Level—Still Rings Culminating Activity.

Activity: Gymnastics   Skill: Balance Beam
Equipment: Balance Beam   Level: Advanced
                                              (blue)

Tasks:
1. Squat Mount—Stand facing the side of the beam placing the hands on the beam. Jump up and forward placing the feet on the beam (between the hands) keeping the body in a squat position. Hold three seconds. Repeat four times. (21)
2. Balance in a piked position (V-sit) while sitting on the beam. Hold three seconds. Repeat twice. (17)
3. Balance on the beam in a squat positon and turn to face the opposite direction while squatting. Repeat five times. (19)
4. Straddle Jump Dismount—Jump off the side of the beam with the legs apart in a straddle position landing to a controlled, balanced position. Repeat four times. (25)

When you have successfully completed all four tasks, move to Advanced (blue) Level—Side Horse Vaulting OR Advanced (blue) Level—Balance Beam Culminating Activity.

Activity: Gymnastics   Skill: Side Horse
                                              Vaulting
Equipment: Side Horse   Level: Advanced
                                              (blue)

Tasks:
1. Squat Vault—Take a run, jump onto the board, hands are placed on the horse while legs are bent (squat) so they can pass between the arms without contacting the horse. The arms push away from the horse and the body is extended before landing. Repeat three times. (12)
2. Straddle Vault—Take a run, jump onto the board getting a lot of height with the hips. Hands are placed on the horse while the legs remain straight and in a straddle position as they pass over the horse without making contact. (Feet are outside of the hands). The arms push away from the horse as the legs are brought together for the landing. Repeat three times. (13)
3. Wolf Vault—Take a run, jump onto the board, hands contact the horse while the legs and body pass over the horse in the wolf position (one leg squatting and the other leg extended straight out to the side). The hands push away from the horse and the legs are brought together for the landing. Repeat three times. (14)
4. Repeat Task #14 to the other side (reverse legs). (15)

When you have successfully completed all four tasks, move to Advanced (blue) Level—Uneven Bars OR Advanced (blue) Level—Side Horse Vaulting Culminating Activity.

Activity: Gymnastics   Skill: Uneven Bars
Equipment: Uneven Bars   Level: Advanced
                                          (blue)

Tasks:
1. Swing to Tuck Mount—Jump to a hang on the high bar using an overgrip. Swing the legs back and forth and then forward with force (tucked position) so both legs can pass over the low bar and the thighs can rest on the low bar. Hold for six seconds. Repeat three times. (3)
2. Front Hip Circle—Execute a front support and shift the body weight forward by leaning forward with the chest. Flex the body at the waist and bend the elbows when inverted for a full body rotation of the bar. Return to the starting position. Repeat four times. (10)
3. Rise to Front Support—Overgrip the high bar with the feet resting on the low bar. Straighten the legs and push down on the high bar with the arms ending in a front support. Hold three seconds. Repeat three times. (11)
4. Pull Over to High Bar—Overgrip the high bar (body facing the low bar) with one leg extended and the other leg bent and resting on the low bar. Swing the extended leg backward and upward over the high bar keeping the arms bent. Push off with the flexed leg and rotate to a front support. Hold three seconds. Repeat three times. (12)
5. Forward Roll Dismount—From a front support on the high or low bar, bend forward at the waist, roll over the bar, and extend the legs down toward the ground. The arms can be released for the dismount. Repeat five times. (5)

When you have successfully completed all five tasks, move to Advanced (blue) Level—Parallel Bars OR Advanced (Blue) Level—Uneven Bars Culminating Activity.

Activity: Gymnastics   Skill: Parallel
                                             Bars
Equipment: Parallel Bars   Level: Advanced
                                             (blue)

Tasks:
1. Straddle Seat Mount—Jump and raise the body to a straddle seat from a straight arm support mount. Hold three seconds. Repeat four times. (16)
2. Skin the Cat—Hold the bars, tuck up the legs and hips and bring them over the head passing through the bars. After lowering the legs, release the hands and drop to a stand. Repeat three times. (10)
3. Side Stride—Execute a straddle seat then quarter turn the body to either side. The body is across the bars with the front knee bent around the bar and the back leg resting on the thigh muscle. Hold three seconds. Repeat three times. (13)
4. Forward Roll—From a straddle seat, reach forward and grasp the bars bending the elbows out to the side. Roll forward by raising the hips, rounding the back, and rolling onto the upper arms. The legs remain straddled so that the thighs land on the bars and roll back into a straddle seat. Repeat four times. (14)
5. Front Vault Dismount—From a straight arm support, swing both legs backward over the bar. Land beside the bars with the hand nearest the bar regripping it. Repeat four times. (18)

When you have successfully completed all five tasks, move to Advanced (blue) Level—Low Horizontal Bar OR Advanced (blue) Level—Parallel Bars Culminating Activity.

Activity: Gymnastics   Skill: Low Horizontal
                                    Bar
Equipment: Low Horizontal Bar   Level: Advanced
                                    (blue)

Tasks:
1. Pull-up—Grasp the bar (overgrip or undergrip) and raise the body so the chin touches the bar. Then lower the body. Do five pull-ups in a row. Repeat twice. (18)
2. Skin the Cat—Grasp the bar (overgrip) and pull the feet up between the arms under the bar. The legs are then lowered and extended toward the ground. This can be used as a dismount by releasing the bar at this point or the legs can be brought back up and over thus reversing the sequence. Repeat three times. (19)
3. Bird's Nest—Grasp the bar (overgrip) and bring both legs up through the arms and hook the knees on the bar. Arch back and slide the legs so the heels rest on the bar. The arms are held straight. Repeat twice. (20)
4. Forward Roll—Execute a front hand support and bend forward at the waist rolling over the bar and causing the legs to extend down toward the ground. Dismount by releasing the bar. Repeat four times. (21)

When you have successfully completed all four tasks, move to Advanced (blue) Level—Still Rings OR Advanced (blue) Level—Low Horizontal Bar Culminating Activity.

Activity: Gymnastics   Skill: Still Rings
Equipment: Set of Rings   Level: Advanced
                                    (blue)

Tasks:
1. Inverted Hang—Execute a tuck position then raise the body upward by straightening the legs over the hands. Dismount by returning to the tuck position and then lowering the legs. Hold the inverted hang three seconds. Repeat twice. (8)
2. Bird's Nest—Execute an inverted hang and hook the toes in the rings so the chest is arched and the head is held high. Hold for three seconds, then return to the inverted position for a dismount. Repeat twice. (10)
3. Skin the Cat Dismount—Execute a flexed arm hang, kick the legs overhead and roll until the legs are extending down. Dismount by releasing the rings at this point. Repeat three times. (12)

When you have successfully completed all three tasks, move to Advanced (blue) Level—Still Rings Culminating Activity.

Culminating Activity Task Cards for Gymnastics

Activity: Gymnastics   Skill: Balance
                                                     Beam
                                                     Culminating
                                                     Activity
Equipment: Balance Beam   Level: Beginner
                                                     (yellow)

Combine several locomotor movements and turns into a routine on the balance beam.

When you have developed your routine, demonstrate it to two other students working on your level.

Activity: Gymnastics   Skill: Balance Beam
                                                     Culminating
                                                     Activity
Equipment: Balance Beam   Level: Intermediate
                                                     (red)

Combine a mount, dismount, and several locomotor movements, turns, and static positions into a routine on the balance beam.

When you have developed your routine, demonstrate it to two other students working at the Intermediate Level.

Activity: Gymnastics   Skill: Balance Beam
                                                     Culminating
                                                     Activity
Equipment: Balance Beam   Level: Advanced
                                                     (blue)

Create a balance beam routine and execute it to music. The routine should last 100 seconds in length and use locomotor movements, turns, and static positions (hold three seconds each) as well as a mount and dismount. (29)

Rehearse your routine and then demonstrate it to the entire class.

Activity: Gymnastics   Skill: Side Horse
Vaulting
Culminating
Activity

Equipment: Side Horse   Level: Beginner
(yellow)

Choose two favorite vaults to perfect. Practice them until they can be executed with control.

Demonstrate the vaults to other students working at the beginning level.

Activity: Gymnastics   Skill: Side Horse
Vaulting
Culminating
Activity

Equipment: Side Horse   Level: Intermediate
(red)

Choose three favorite vaults to perfect. Focus attention on smoothness and balance on your landing.

Demonstrate the vaults to other students working at the intermediate level.

Activity: Gymnastics   Skill: Side Horse
Vaulting
Culminating
Activity

Equipment: Side Horse   Level: Advanced
(blue)

Choose three vaults to perfect with one being of increased difficulty. Concentrate on a balanced landing with the feet remaining together and with any extra steps being avoided. The arms should be placed in a "V-position" above the head. This stance should be held (pause) before leaving the mat where the landing occurred. (18)

After working on the three vaults, demonstrate them to the entire class.

Activity:	Gymnastics	Skill:	Uneven Bars Culminating Activity
Equipment:	Uneven Bars	Level:	Beginner (yellow)

Choose several uneven bar stunts and combine them into a routine. The stunts should be chosen so that smoothness and continuity is achieved when moving from one stunt to another.

Demonstrate the uneven bar routine to two students working at the beginner level.

Activity:	Gymnastics	Skill:	Uneven Bars Culminating Activity
Equipment:	Uneven Bars	Level:	Intermediate (red)

Choose several uneven bar stunts including a mount and a dismount and combine them into a routine. Integration and flow from one stunt to another is important.

Demonstrate the uneven bar routine to two students working at the intermediate level.

Activity:	Gymnastics	Skill:	Uneven Bars Culminating Activity
Equipment:	Uneven Bars	Level:	Advanced (blue)

Execute the following bar routine:
  Mount to a front support (hold three seconds).
  Swan balance (three seconds).
  Front hip circle.
  Pull over to high bar (hold front support three seconds).
  Forward roll dismount. (16)

Demonstrate the routine to the other students working at the advanced level.

Activity: Gymnastics   Skill: Parallel
                                              Bars
                                              Culminating
                                              Activity
Equipment: Parallel Bars   Level: Beginner
                                              (yellow)

Choose several parallel bars stunts and combine them into a routine. The stunts should be executed with smoothness and continuity.

Demonstrate the parallel bars routine to two students working at the beginner level.

Activity: Gymnastics   Skill: Parallel
                                              Bars
                                              Culminating
                                              Activity
Equipment: Parallel Bars   Level: Intermediate
                                              (red)

Combine a mount, several stunts, and a dismount into a routine on the parallel bars. Attention should be given to smooth transition from one stunt to another.

Demonstrate the parallel bar routine to two students working at the intermediate level.

Activity: Gymnastics   Skill: Parallel Bars
                                              Culminating
                                              Activity
Equipment: Parallel Bars   Level: Advanced
                                              (blue)

Perform the following routine:
   Straight arm support mount (hold three seconds).
   Hand walk backward halfway across the bars.
   Straddle seat (hold three seconds).
   Side stride (hold three seconds).
   Straddle travel to the end of the bars.
   Front vault dismount. (20)

Demonstrate the routine to the entire class when it has been perfected.

Activity: Gymnastics   Skill: Low Horizontal
                                                Bar
                                                Culminating
                                                Activity

Equipment: Low Horizontal Bar   Level: Beginner
                                                (yellow)

Choose several low horizontal bar stunts and combine into a routine.
The routine should be practiced until the stunts flow smoothly from
one stunt to another.

Demonstrate your routine to two students working at the beginner
level.

Activity: Gymnastics   Skill: Low
                                                Horizontal Bar
                                                Culminating
                                                Activity

Equipment: Low Horizontal Bar   Level: Intermediate
                                                (red)

Choose several low horizontal bar stunts and combine into a routine.
The stunts should be chosen so that smoothness and continuity are
achieved when moving from one stunt to another.

Demonstrate your routine to two students working at the intermediate
level.

Activity: Gymnastics   Skill: Low
                                                Horizontal Bar
                                                Culminating
                                                Activity

Equipment: Low Horizontal Bar   Level: Advanced
                                                (blue)

Execute the following low horizontal bar routine:
    Mount to a flexed arm hang (hold three seconds).
    Front swing back and forth three times.
    One knee hang (hold three seconds).
    One knee mount (hold stride three seconds).
    Front hand support (hold three seconds).
    Forward roll dismount. (22)

Demonstrate the routine to the entire class when you have perfected
it.

Activity: Gymnastics   Skill: Still Rings
                                                   Culminating
                                                   Activity
Equipment: Set of Rings   Level: Beginner
                                                   (yellow)

Combine several ring stunts into a routine. The rings should be held
quite motionless throughout the routine.

Demonstrate the routine to two students working at the beginner
level.

Activity: Gymnastics   Skill: Still Rings
                                                   Culminating
                                                   Activity
Equipment: Set of Rings   Level: Intermediate
                                                   (red)

Choose several still ring stunts and combine into a routine. The stunts
should be chosen so that smoothness and continuity are achieved
when moving from one stunt to another.

Demonstrate the routine to two students working at the intermediate
level.

Activity: Gymnastics   Skill: Still Rings
                                                   Culminating
                                                   Activity
Equipment: Set of Rings   Level: Advanced
                                                   (blue)

Execute the following still rings routine:
    Mount to a flexed arm hang (hold three seconds).
    Do three pull-ups.
    Inverted hang (hold three seconds).
    Bird's nest (hold three seconds).
    Flexed arm hang (hold three seconds).
    Skin the cat dismount. (13)

Demonstrate the following routine to the entire class after devoting
time to perfecting it.

SOCCER MINI-UNIT

Activity: Soccer   Skill: Dribble
Equipment: Soccer Ball   Level: Beginner
                                                (yellow)

Tasks:
1. Dribble the width of the field two times using inside of foot dribble. (1)
2. Repeat Task #1 using a zigzag pathway. (2)
3. Repeat Tasks #1 and #2 using the outside of foot dribble. (4)
4. Repeat Tasks #1 and #2 using a toe dribble. (5)

When you have successfully completed all four tasks, move to Beginner (yellow) Level—Kick Pass.

Activity: Soccer   Skill: Kick-Pass
Equipment: Soccer Ball   Level: Beginner
                                                (yellow)

Tasks:
1. Kick into a wall target 10 times using each kind of kick (inside of foot, toe, and outside of foot) from a stationary position. (1)
2. Repeat Task #1 hitting the target five out of 10 times with each kick. (2)
3. Repeat Tasks #1 and #2 from a three step approach. (3)
4. From a stationary position, kick at a pin (use all kicks). Complete five out of 10, seven out of 10 successful hits. (4)

When you have successfully completed all four tasks, move to Beginner (yellow) Level—Trap.

Activity: Soccer   Skill: Trap
Equipment: Soccer Ball   Level: Beginner
                                                    (yellow)

Tasks:
1. Kick the ball into the wall and trap rebound with the sole of the foot. Repeat until successful five consecutive times. (1)
2. Kick the ball into the wall and trap rebound with the inside of the leg. Repeat until successful five consecutive times. (2)
3. Kick the ball into the wall and trap rebound with the inside of both legs or front of both legs. Repeat until successful five consecutive times.

When you have successfully completed all three tasks, move to Beginner (yellow) Level—Tackle.

Activity: Soccer   Skill: Tackle
Equipment: Soccer Ball   Level: Beginner
                                                    (yellow)

Tasks:
1. In partners and with one soccer ball, play Keep Away in a 10 to 15-foot area for three minutes. Rules prohibit body contact and kicking the ball out of the designated area. (1)
2. In partners, A dribbles toward B who executes a front tackle. Reverse. Repeat three times. (2)

When you have successfully completed both tasks, move to Beginner (yellow) Level—Culminating Activity OR to Intermediate (red) Level—Dribble.

Activity: Soccer

Skill: Culminating Activity

Equipment: Soccer Ball

Level: Beginner (yellow)

Play the game "Line Kick" as described by Blake and Volp (1964, p.96). The players are numbered on each team and the two teams line up facing each other. When a number is called the player from each team runs forward and tries to get possession of the ball so it can be returned to the linemen of his own team. The linemen (the only ones allowed to score a point) then try to kick the ball below the shoulders through the other line. After each score a different number is called.

When you have played "Line Kick" for 15 minutes, move to Intermediate (red) Level—Dribble.

Activity: Soccer
Equipment: Soccer Ball

Skill: Dribble
Level: Intermediate (red)

Tasks:
1. Dribble through Indian club obstacles using the inside of foot dribble. (6)
2. Repeat Task #1 using a toe dribble. (7)
3. Repeat Task #1 and # 2 for time. Record the best time from two trials. (8)

When you have successfully completed all three tasks, move to Intermediate (red) Level—Kick-Pass.

Activity: Soccer
Equipment: Soccer Ball

Skill: Kick-Pass
Level: Intermediate (red)

Tasks:
1. In partners while moving, combine a dribble and kick-pass to a moving partner who is to your right, left, and diagonally ahead of you. Reverse. (8)
2. In partners, complete five successful kick-passes while moving at maximum speed across the width of the field. (10)

When you have successfully completed all three tasks, move to Intermediate (red) Level—Trap.

Activity: Soccer   Skill: Trap
Equipment: Soccer Ball   Level: Intermediate
                                                  (red)

Tasks:
1. In partners, A rolls the ball toward B and calls the kind of trap. B
    traps. Roll the ball 10 times. Reverse. (4)
2. In partners, A bounces the ball toward B. B traps using inside of
    front of both legs. Repeat 10 times. Reverse. (5)
3. Repeat Tasks #1 and #2 with the ball being rolled or bounced to
    both sides. (6)

When you have successfully completed all three tasks, move to
Intermediate (red) Level—Tackle.

Activity: Soccer   Skill: Tackle
Equipment: Soccer Ball   Level: Intermediate
                                                  (red)

Tasks:
1. In threes, A dribbles toward B who executes a front tackle and
    immediately passes to C. Rotate. Repeat five times. (5)
2. Repeat Task #1 using a hook tackle instead of a front tackle. (8)

When you have successfully completed both tasks, move to
Intermediate (red) Level—Volley.

Activity: Soccer   Skill: Volley
Equipment: Soccer Ball   Level: Intermediate
                                                  (red)

Tasks:
1. In partners, A throws the ball toward B's shoulder and B volleys
    the ball executing a shoulder volley. Repeat five times from a
    distance of 10 feet. Reverse. (1)
2. Repeat Task #1 executing a knee volley. (4)
3. Repeat Task #1 executing a foot volley. (5)
4   In partners, A throws the ball underhand so that it arches and
    drops toward B's head. B executes a head volley. Repeat three
    times from a distance of 10 feet. Reverse. (6)

When you have successfully completed all four tasks, move to
Intermediate (red) Level—Block.

Activity: Soccer Skill: Block
Equipment: Soccer Ball Level: Intermediate
(red)

Tasks:
1. In partners, A throws the ball toward B's chest and B blocks the ball executing a chest block. (1)
2. Repeat Task #1 using a leg block.
3. Repeat Task #1 using a foot block.

When you have successfully completed all three tasks, move to Intermediate (red) Level—Punt and Drop Kick.

Activity: Soccer Skill: Punt and Drop Kick
Equipment: Soccer Ball Level: Intermediate
(red)

Tasks:
1. Punt five balls from a stationary position. (2)
2. Punt five balls from a moving position. Use one or two steps. (3)
3. Punt three balls a minimum of 25 yards. (4)
4. Repeat Tasks #1-3 using a drop kick. (9)

When you have successfully completed all four tasks, move to Intermediate (red) Level—Culminating Activity OR Advanced (blue) Level—Dribble.

Activity: Soccer Skill: Culminating Activity
Equipment: Soccer Ball Level: Intermediate
(red)

Play the game "Rotation Soccer" as described by Blake and Volp (1964, p. 103). Two teams are made up of equal groups of forwards, guards, and goalies. A point is scored when a forward kicks the ball over the other team's end line below shoulder level. The forwards play in the opponent's half of the field and the guards play on their own half. The goalies remain on the end line to defend their goal. (They may use their hands.) Whenever a point is scored, the positions are rotated and the team scored against kicks off.

When you have played "Rotation Soccer" for 15 minutes, move to Advanced (blue) Level—Dribble.

Activity: Soccer   Skill: Dribble
Equipment: Soccer ball   Level: Advanced
                                                    (blue)

Tasks:
1. Dribble in a straight pathway and on signal (whistle) change direction or pathway. Continue the width of the soccer field (110 yards).
2. Dribble in a straight pathway and on signal (whistle) dribble in a circular pathway combining inside and outside of foot dribbling. Continue the width of the soccer field. (10)
3. In partners and moving in the same direction, A dribbles 8-10 feet and passes diagonally ahead to B who dribbles and passes diagonally ahead of A. Continue the length of the soccer field. (13)

When you have successfully completed all three tasks, move to Advanced (blue) Level—Kick—Pass.

Activity: Soccer   Skills: Kick-Pass
Equipment: Soccer Ball   Level: Advanced
                                                    (blue)

Tasks:
1. Dribble from 25-yard line and kick for goal. Score three consecutive goals. Kick from center, diagonal right, and diagonal left positions. (14)
2. In partners, dribble and pass from 50-yard line and kick for goal. Complete successful passes and goals three out of five times. (15)
3. In groups of three, A and B pass and dribble from the 50-yard line and kick for goals. C plays goalie and defends the goal. Complete successful passes and goal two out of five times. (16)

When you have successfully completed all three tasks, move to Advanced (blue) Level—Trap.

Activity: Soccer   Skill: Trap
Equipment: Soccer Ball   Level: Advanced (blue)

Tasks:
1. In partners, A kicks the ball toward B. B traps five times with inside of one leg. Repeat with the other leg. Reverse. (7)
2. Repeat Task #1 using the inside or front of both legs. (8)
3. Repeat Task #1 using the sole of foot trap. (9)
4. In partners, A kicks the ball to right side of B. B traps and kicks the ball back to A who traps. Trap 10 balls using a variety of traps. Repeat to the left side. (10)

When you have successfully completed all four tasks, move to Advanced (blue) Level—Tackle.

Activity: Soccer   Skill: Tackle
Equipment: Soccer Ball   Level: Advanced (blue)

Tasks:
1. In partners, A dribbles while B moves alongside of A. B executes a side tackle and dribbles back toward the starting point. Reverse. Repeat three times. (9)
2. In two teams of two each, Team A dribbles and passes toward opponents, Team B, who tries to tackle executing a front or hook tackle. A marked neutral area can be used so that points can be awarded to the team who moves the ball out of the neutral zone. Play continues for 10 minutes. (12)

When you have successfully completed both tasks, move to Advanced (blue) Level—Volley.

Activity: Soccer   Skill: Volley
Equipment: Soccer Ball   Level: Advanced (blue)

Tasks:
1. In partners, A throws the ball toward B's foot, knee, shoulder, or head and B volleys the ball to the left, right, and toward the center. Repeat 10 times. (1)
2. Stand 10 to 15 feet from a wall and kick the ball into the wall. Volley the rebound with different body parts (foot, knee, shoulder, and head) according to the level of rebound. Repeat 10 times. (8)

When you have successfully completed both tasks, move to Advanced (blue) Level—Block.

Activity: Soccer   Skill: Block
Equipment: Soccer Ball   Level: Advanced
                                            (blue)

Tasks:
1. Stand 10 to 15 feet from a wall and kick the ball into the wall. Block the rebound with different body parts (chest, abdomen, thighs, leg, or foot) according to the level of rebound. Repeat 10 times.
2. In partners and from a distance of 10-15 feet, A lifts the ball while passing to B who uses different body parts to block the ball. Reverse and repeat 10 times. (2)

When you have successfully completed both tasks, move to Advanced (blue) Level—Punt and Drop Kick.

Activity: Soccer   Skill: Punt
                                            Drop Kick
Equipment: Soccer Ball   Level: Advanced
                                            (blue)

Tasks:
1. From a goalie's position, punt three balls toward the left alley. Repeat toward the right alley and down the center. (6)
2. In partners, A kicks the ball toward B who picks the ball up and punts. Repeat 10 times and reverse. (7)
3. Repeat Tasks #1 and #2 using a drop kick. (9)

When you have successfully completed all three tasks, move to Advanced (blue) Level—Culminating Activity.

Activity: Soccer   Skill: Culminating
                                            Activity
Equipment: Soccer Ball   Level: Advanced
                                            (blue)

Play a soccer game.

Continue play for set time period.

BADMINTON UNIT

(Supervised Task Programming Model)

The badminton unit is planned for 25-30 students in a facility that provides four courts and wall space. During the early days in the unit, two courts or less may need to be set up. Plans for allowing several students to complete tasks in the same area can be organized at the discretion of the teacher. For example, four students or two sets of partners could be practicing short serves while four other students could be practicing deep clears on the same court.

Game play can be modified by shortening the number of points to win or using time instead of points. If the number of courts and students exceeds the limits for completion of the learning packet, singles play could be eliminated or extra playing time could be arranged before and after school or during lunch hour.

This unit is planned for 20 days which may or may not agree with the teacher's schedule. Therefore, modifications would be necessary.

The teacher may question why tests are programmed before the completion of the unit. Our rationale is that information gained through testing can still be incorporated into the learning process and aid in the development of game skills.

General instructions to the Teacher:

- Plan to utilize all space well. Many tasks can be completed in small areas and programmed concurrently.
- Keep all students busy and on-task. At first they will tend to drift or wait to be directed. This is especially true if students have not previously been exposed to this method.
- Move around, observe student performance, and provide evaluative feedback and encouragement. Interaction is vital to the success of this method.
- Conduct spot checks on student performance early in the unit. This will tend to keep students more responsible.
- Teach the next master lesson when the majority of the students have completed over half of the tasks on the present skill lesson. Master lessons can be given anytime during the lesson and need not initiate the lesson.
- Make use of chalkboards for additional directions, announcements, and general information. This keeps class interruptions to a minimum and promotes student responsibility for gaining information.
- Organize the activity environment to ensure good safety practices.
- Designate an area(s) for getting and returning badminton rackets, shuttles, nets, and standards.

- Take time the first day of the unit to orient students to the overall plan of the unit. Go over the contract but do not have students complete it until they begin day three.
- If the gymnasium lacks adequate space for loop films, books, and articles, an alternative center could be planned in the library or instructional center.

BADMINTON LEARNING PACKET

INTRODUCTION

The Badminton Learning Packet is your workbook for this unit of instruction. You will be working on different levels of badminton skills progressing from easier to harder learning tasks. Later in the unit you will use various skills in game play. Throughout this unit, I encourage you to practice and learn the skills and game of badminton to the best of your ability. Relax and enjoy yourself.

General Expectations, Instructions and Procedures
1. You are expected to come to class dressed in tennis shoes, socks, shorts, and shirt.
2. You are expected to contract and complete the cognitive, psychomotor, and affective task learning experiences at a passing grade level and at the "pass" level where so designated.
3. You are expected to help with the setting up and taking down of equipment. Please register for three days by signing your name to the sheet located on the bulletin board. On your assigned days, come quickly to the gym so that the equipment is ready for the class.
4. You will have your own Badminton Learning Packet. At the beginning of class you will remove it from the large envelope which is arranged alphabetically in the file box. At the end of class you will return it. A box of pencils is located near the file box.
5. Practice and complete the tasks in progressive order, both on each task sheet and succeeding task sheets. The packet is designed to let each of you practice and learn at your own rate of speed.
6. Be aware of your task sheet completion dates and pace yourself accordingly.
7. Master lessons on skills and game play will be given according to the schedule. After each lesson, practice and complete 3-5 tasks before going back to your previous task sheet(s).
8. At the end of the Badminton Learning Packet you will find:
   8.1 A skill analysis for each badminton skill. This information will aid in your understanding of how the skill is performed.
   8.2 Loop film task sheets.
9. The organization of the class is individualized. You are expected to practice your tasks alone or with others according to the task instructions. If you need to work with a partner, try to find someone who is working on a similar task so that you can benefit each other.
10. This unit is *not* a race. Do not hurry through your tasks. Take your time and do each one well.

11. You may change your contract only on the 5th and 10th day of the unit.
12. I may request a check of your skills at any time.
13. The following items are located on the table at the south side of the stage.
    13.1 File box of student workbooks
    13.2 Box of pencils
    13.3 Box containing rope, tape, chalk
    13.4 Loop film projector and loop films
    13.5 Badminton books and articles
    13.6 Hoops
    All items are to be taken from and returned to their designated areas/containers.
14. I am here to help you. If you are having difficulty, seek my assistance immediately.

20 DAY UNIT GUIDE

The first column announces the day and activity when a master lesson will be given and testing days. The second column announces the day when task sheets for the skill/activity are to be completed.

	Task Initiation	**Task Completion**
Day 1	Clear	
2	Serve	
3		
4	Smash	Clear
5		
6	Drop	Serve
7		
8	Net	
9	Drive	Smash
10	Terminology Quiz	Drop
11	Doubles Play	
12		
13		Net
14		Drive
15	Singles Play	
16	Final Written Test	
17		
18		
19		
20		Rest of Tasks

BADMINTON CONTRACT

I agree to complete the bookwork, Badminton Learning Packet, at the _____ percent level which is a letter grade of _____ . I assume the responsibility for completing the task sheets, taking tests, checking my classmates' tasks, and helping with equipment. I am aware that I can change my contract on the 5th and 10th day of this unit. I understand that the grade that I am contracting for will only be given if I complete all assignments that are consistent with the level of performance expectation.

_____   _____
Student   Date

_____   _____
Teacher   Date

GRADING

90% and above = A—
Complete 90% or more tasks on each task sheet. Score 90% or better on all tests. Evaluate classmates' performance correctly. Help with equipment. Return all equipment and materials to designated areas.

80% to 89% = B—
Complete 80-89% of tasks on each task sheet. Score 80-89% on all tests. Evaluate classmates' performance correctly. Help with equipment. Return all equipment and materials to designated areas.

70% to 79% = C—
Complete 70-79% of tasks on each task sheet. Score 70-79% on all tests. Evaluate classmates' performance correctly. Help with equipment. Return all equipment and materials to designated areas.

60% to 69% = D —
Complete 60-69% of tasks on each task sheet. Score 60-69% on all tests. Evaluate classmates' performance correctly. Help with equipment. Return all equipment and materials to designated areas.

TASK SHEET—CLEAR

STUDENT _____

Tasks #1-9-11-15 to be checked by instructor. Tasks #2-3-7-8-10-12-16 are to be checked and initialed by a peer. The rest of the tasks are to be self checked.

TASK LEARNING EXPERIENCES	EVALUATION		
	SELF	PEER	INSTR.
1. View overhead forehand strokes loop film. Complete loop task sheet.			
2. In partners, A takes a forehand grip and B assesses the grip according to the skill analysis. Reverse.			
3. Repeat task #2 using a backhand grip.			
4. Swing the racket for a clear 10 times. Concentrate on a forceful swing. Listen for a swishing sound			
5. Self toss a shuttle high and clear against a wall. Repeat 10 times from a distance of 20 feet. Concentrate on timing and force.			
6. In partners, A tosses high shuttles to B who clears against a wall. Repeat 10 times clearing from a distance of 20 feet and reverse. Increase distance to 30 feet, 35 feet, 40 feet.		P	C
7. Repeat task #6 and record number of hits against the wall out of 5 trials. Pass level: 4 at 20', 3 at 30', 2 at 35', 1 at 40'. Challenge level: (optional) 5 at 20', 4 at 30', 3 at 35', 2 at 40'.	20 feet 30 feet 35 feet 40 feet		
		P	C
8. Repeat tasks #5, 6 and 7 using an underhand clear with 5 trials each. Record for task #7 in the right column.	20 feet 30 feet 35 feet 40 feet		
9. Stand at the service line for doubles and self toss the shuttle high and clear over the net to the back court area. Repeat 5 times.			
10. Repeat task #9 recording the number of clears that land between the service line for doubles and the line for singles (6 inches either side is O.K.). Take 10 trials. Pass level: 4 out of 10—record. Challenge level: (optional) 7 out of 10—record.	P # C #		

TASK LEARNING EXPERIENCES	EVALUATION		
	SELF	PEER	INSTR.
11. Repeat task #9 using an underhand clear.			
12. Repeat task #10 using an underhand clear. Pass level: 4 out of 10—record. Challenge level: (optional) 7 out of 10—record.	P # C #		
13. In partners, A serves high and deep to B who clears to back area of court. Repeat 10 times and reverse.			
14. Repeat task #13 using a backhand clear.			
15. In partners, A and B stand about 30 feet apart and rally (about 3-4 times) using combinations of overhand, backhand, and underhand clears. Continue by increasing the distance to 35 and 40 feet.			
16. In partners, each stands behind service line for doubles and clears. Rally counting consecutive clears. Do not count if either must take more than one step over the line and into the court to clear. Record the highest number in 3 trials.	# Consecutive _____		

SUMMARY
1. _____ Number of tasks completed.
2. _____ Task or tasks that were the most difficult.
3. _____ Check the number of tasks completed.
           _____ 14 or more
           _____ 12-13
           _____ 11
           _____ 9-10
           _____ 8 or less

TASK SHEET—SERVE

STUDENT _____

Tasks #3-8-9-15-16-19 are to be checked by instructor. Tasks #2-14-17-18 are to be checked and initialed by a peer. The rest of the tasks are to be self-checked.

TASK LEARNING EXPERIENCES	EVALUATION		
	SELF	PEER	INSTR.
1. Serve 10 shuttles against the green wall concentrating on the timing of the drop and swing. Stand behind the first yellow line.			
2. Repeat task #1 concentrating on the mechanics and rules governing the serve; then get a partner and each assess the other according to the rules.			
3. Repeat #1 serving above a 5' line on the wall. Serve until you are successful 5 consecutive times.			
4. Repeat task #3 serving 10 shuttles between the 5 & 7 foot line on the wall. Pass level: 5 out of 10. Record number. Do not move to task #5 until successful.	P#		
5. Stand in the front inside corner area of a court without a net & serve 10 shuttles into a legal court diagonally across from your court. Check wall chart for lines and areas. Remain at station until 10 legally fall into the opposite court.			
6. Repeat task #5 serving into the front one-third of the court.			
7. Repeat task #5 serving into the back one third of the court.			
8. Repeat tasks #6 & 7 from a center court serving position. What kind of adjustments are necessary to produce differing amounts of force. Write in space below.			
9. Repeat tasks #5, 6, & 7 on a court with a net at the legal height.			
10. Repeat tasks #6 & 7 from the adjacent court.			
11. Serve 5 shuttles short & low into different areas of the front singles court. Doubles court.			
12. Serve 5 shuttles long & high into different areas of the back singles court. Doubles court.			
13. Stretch a rope 2' above & parallel to the top of the net. Serve 10 shuttles between the net and rope and into the front court. Pass level: 4 out of 10. Challenge level: (optional) 8 out of 10 —record.	P #		
	C #		

TASK LEARNING EXPERIENCES	EVALUATION		
	SELF	PEER	INSTR.

14. In partners, A serves to B who returns the serve. Serve 5 & reverse. Complete 5 trials. DO NOT RALLY.

15. Repeat task #14 serving to different court areas. Discuss & write which service areas are the most difficult to return. Easiest. Write in space below.

16. In partners, A serves to B who tries to smash the return. Serve a mixture of placements. Serve 10 & reverse. Discuss & write where the best areas are to avoid a smash return. Write in space below.

17. In partners, serve adding a scoring element. Score one point for the server on a legal return. Score one point for the receiver if the server fails to complete a legal serve and when the receiver returns a serve legally. Continue until either scores 10 points. DO NOT RALLY.

18. In partners, A serves, B returns and A returns. Serve 5 times and reverse. Discuss serving strategies for best possible court position for returning the serve and then for A's return. Check your discussion points by repeating serve, return, return.

19. Repeat task #1 using the backhand low serve.

20. Repeat tasks #3 and 4 using the backhand low serve.

21. Repeat tasks #5, 6 and 7 using the backhand low service. Pass level: 3 out of 10. Challenge level: (optional) 7 out of 10.

22. Repeat task #13 using the backhand low service. Pass level: 3 out of 10. Challenge level: 7 out of 10.

23. Repeat task #17 using the backhand low service.

	P	C
#5		
#6		
#7		
P #		
C #		

SUMMARY
1. _____ Number of tasks completed.
2. _____ Task or tasks that were the most difficult.
3. _____ Check the number of tasks completed.
   _____ 20 or more
   _____ 18-19
   _____ 16-17
   _____ 13-15
   _____ 12 or less

TASK SHEET—SMASH

STUDENT _____

Tasks #1 and 13 to be checked by instructor. Tasks #3,5,6,9,10 are to be checked and initialed by a peer. The rest of the tasks are to be self-checked.

TASK LEARNING EXPERIENCES	EVALUATION		
	SELF	PEER	INSTR.
1. Stand 10 feet from a wall and self-toss the shuttle high. Hit the shuttle against the bottom of the wall. Repeat 10 times.			
2. Repeat task #1. Stand a hula hoop against the wall and smash shuttle into hoop. Score 3 out of 10, 5 out of 10.			
3. In partners about 15 feet apart, A tosses the shuttle high to B who tries to hit and direct it forcefully at A's feet. Reverse after 10 trials. Together discuss and write in space below. 3.1 In order to direct the shuttle at your partner's feet, where, in relation to the body, did you contact the shuttle? 3.2 What was the angle of the racket face on contact? Repeat 2 more trials of 5 shuttles each and note the above questions.			
4. View loop film and answer loop film task sheet on smash.			
5. In partners, and on a court with a net in between, A tosses the shuttle high to racket side of B who smashes. Repeat 10 times and reverse. Repeat again and concentrate on directing the smash between service line and net or hitting your partner between the hips and feet. Pass level: 3 out of 10.	P #		
6. Repeat task #5 with A tossing high to non-racket side of B who uses a backhand smash. Pass level: 2 out of 10.	P #		
7. In partners, A tosses the shuttle high to different areas of the court. B smashes. Reverse. Discuss and write in space below. 7.1 From what areas of the court were you most successful in smashing?			

	EVALUATION		
TASK LEARNING EXPERIENCES	SELF	PEER	INSTR.
7.2 How would you relate this to your opponent's chance of returning a smash?			
8. Repeat task #7 with A serving a high shuttle to B who smashes and A tries to return the smash. Repeat 10 times and reverse. Discuss again the questions in task #7.			
9. In partners, A serves high shuttles to B who smashes to various areas of the court. Repeat 10 times and reverse. Note the angle of the racket face at contact.			
10. Repeat task #9 placing 4 out of 10 down right side of court. Pass level: 4 out of 10 down right side of court.	P #		
	P #		
11. Repeat task #9 with 4 floor targets—(hula hoops) arranged on the court. Give 1 point for each shuttle that lands in a hoop. Best of 10 trials.	#		
12. In partners, A serves the shuttle high to B who smashes to A's forehand side 5 times and to A's backhand 5 times. A tries to return each smash. Reverse. From which side was it more difficult to return the smash? Why?			
13. In groups of four, rally and use the smash whenever the shuttle is high and in the front half of the court. Play for 5 minutes.			

SUMMARY
1. _____ Number of tasks completed.
2. _____ Task or tasks that were the most difficult.
3. _____ Check the number of tasks completed.
            _____ 11 or more
            _____ 10
            _____ 9
            _____ 7-8
            _____ 6 or less

TASK SHEET—DROP

STUDENT _____

Tasks #1 and 12 are to be checked by the instructor. Tasks #5,6,8, and 9 are to be checked and initialed by a peer. The rest of the tasks are to be self-checked.

TASK LEARNING EXPERIENCES	EVALUATION		
	SELF	PEER	INSTR.
1. View loop film on drop and complete loop film task sheet.			
2. Self-toss the shuttle high and hit a drop shot concentrating on the point of contact and checking the swing. Repeat 10 times.			
3. In partners, A tosses the shuttle high to B who assumes the same movement patterns as a clear but returns a drop shot. Toss 10 shuttles and reverse. Concentrate on reducing the speed of the racket and angling the racket face slightly downward on contact.			
4. Repeat task #2 from the front area of the court. Place 10 drop shots as close to the other side of the net as possible. Repeat from a center court position.			
5. Repeat task #3 on a court with A serving high shuttles to B who is hitting from the front area of the court. Try to place the shuttles as close to the other side of the net as possible. Repeat from a center court position. Repeat from the back court position.			
6. Repeat task #5 placing 3 out of 10 between the net and service line. Placing 5/10. Placing 7/10.			
7. Repeat tasks #2-6 using a backhand drop shot.			
8. In partners, A serves high deep shuttles to B who is positioned in the back court. Try to place the shuttle as close to the other side of the net as possible. Reverse after successfully returning 5 shuttles. Each complete 3 trials.			
9. Repeat task #8 using a backhand drop shot.			
10. In partners, rally mixing the drop and clear. Continue 4-5 minutes and concentrate on deceiving your opponent.			
11. Repeat task #5 from the front and center court area mixing the drop and smash shot. Add the smash when appropriate.			

	EVALUATION		
TASK LEARNING EXPERIENCES	SELF	PEER	INSTR.
12. In groups of four, rally 5 minutes using the drop, clear and smash shot. Concentrate on using the same mechanics for all three shots. Try to deceive your opponents.			

SUMMARY
1. _____ Number of tasks completed.
2. _____ Task or tasks that were the most difficult.
3. _____ Check the number of tasks completed.
> _____ 11 or more
> _____ 9 or 10
> _____ 8
> _____ 7
> _____ 6 or less

TASK SHEET—NET SHOTS

STUDENT _____

Task #12 is to be checked by the instructor. Tasks #6,7,8,9,11,12 are to be checked and initialed by a peer. The rest of the tasks are to be self-checked.

TASK LEARNING EXPERIENCES	EVALUATION		
	SELF	PEER	INSTR.
1. Mark 2 parallel lines, 5 feet and 6 feet on the green wall. Stand w/left shoulder toward the wall and about 3-4 feet from it. Self drop shuttles from above the 5 foot line. Guide and direct the shuttle between the lines and *gently* against the wall. If the shuttle rebounds more than 2 feet from the wall, reduce the force of the swing.			
2. Repeat task #1 recording the number of good hits in 3-4 minutes. Do not count rebounds of more than 2 feet.	#		
3. Repeat task #1 scoring 5 consecutive hits.			
4. Repeat tasks #1 and 3 by standing and facing the wall.			
5. Repeat tasks #1 and 3 by standing with the right shoulder to the wall. Toss shuttle instead of dropping it.			
6. In partners and on a court, A tosses shuttles just over the net and in front of the service line to B's forehand side. B returns with an underhand net shot. Concentrate on returning close to the top of the net and in front of the service line. Repeat 5 times and reverse. Complete 3 trials.			
7. Repeat task #6 until each partner is successful 5 times.			
8. Repeat tasks #6 and 7 tossing to the backhand side.			
9. Repeat tasks #6 and 7 with A serving instead of tossing.			
10. Repeat task #9 concentrating on angled flight patterns mixing straight up and down shots with cross court shots.			
11. Stretch a rope 18 inches above and parallel to the top of the net. In partners, A and B assume a position between the net and the service line on opposite sides. Rally net shots for 3 minutes and count the number of placements between the rope and net that qualify as net shots.			

TASK LEARNING EXPERIENCES	EVALUATION		
	SELF	PEER	INSTR.
12. Use the same apparatus and positions in task #11. Continue to hit net shots between the rope and net. Failure to place the shot between the net and rope, and failure to return the shot legally result in a point for your partner. Continue for 3 minutes. Record your score. _____			
13. In partners, A serves short and low to B who returns a net shot. Serve 5 and reverse. Continue for 5 trials.			
14. In groups of four, rally for 5 minutes and use net shots whenever appropriate.			

SUMMARY
1. _____ Number of tasks completed.
2. _____ Task or tasks that were the most difficult.
3. _____ Check the number of tasks completed.
       _____ 12 or more
       _____ 11
       _____ 9-10
       _____ 8
       _____ 7 or less

TASK SHEET—DRIVE

STUDENT _____

Tasks #1 and 9 are to be checked by instructor. Tasks #6,7,8,10, and 11 are to be checked and initialed by a peer. The rest of the tasks are to be self checked.

TASK LEARNING EXPERIENCES	EVALUATION		
	SELF	PEER	INSTR.
1. View loop film on the drive and complete film task sheet.			
2. Swing the racket 5 times using a forehand drive. Concentrate on the mechanics of the swing. Listen for a swishing sound. Repeat using a backhand drive.			
3. Stand about 10 feet from a wall and self toss a shuttle. Hit using a forehand drive. Repeat 10 times. Concentrate on producing a forceful drive and keeping the shuttle flight parallel to the floor and about 5 to 7 feet high.			
4. Repeat task #3 directing the flight to hit above a marked line 5 feet high on the wall.			
5. Repeat tasks #3 and 4 using a backhand drive.			
6. Extend a rope 2 feet above the net. In partners, A and B rally for 4-5 minutes from center court positions using forehand drives. Concentrate on powerful strokes and maintaining a parallel to the floor flight pattern. Pass level: Complete 5 drives each between net and rope. Challenge level: (optional) complete as many as possible.	P # C #		
7. Repeat task #6 using backhand drives.	P # C #		
8. Repeat tasks #6 and 7 with A and B in opposite diagonal courts so that all hits are crosscourt drives.	P # C #		
9. In groups of four, each assumes a center court position. Rally for 5 minutes using the forehand and backhand drive. Concentrate on placing the drives either crosscourt or down the line.			
10. Repeat task #9 adding a scoring method.			
11. In groups of four, rally by combining a mixture of strokes with the drive.			

SUMMARY
1. _____ Number of tasks completed.
2. _____ Task or tasks that were the most difficult.
3. _____ Check the number of tasks completed.
       _____ 10 or more
       _____ 9
       _____ 7-8
       _____ 6
       _____ 5 or less

CHALLENGE TASK SHEET
(Additional credit may be earned; see your teacher.)

Tasks #6-7 are to be checked by the instructor. Tasks #1,2,3,4,5, and 8 are to be checked and initialed by a peer.

	PEER	INSTR.

1. In partners, A serves deep, B returns with an overhead drop shot and A returns with an underhand clear. Place drop shots between net and service line and clears between long service lines. Continue to clear and drop. If court space is limited, a half court can be used. Score 1 point for each successful placement. Rotate after each score. 5 points.

2. Repeat task #1 using backhand drops and clears. After achieving some success, mix forehands and backhands, returning to center court position after each stroke.

3. In partners, A and B play all shots between the net and short service line and the doubles side line. Rally until one player reaches 5 points. Score a point whenever partner doesn't return shot within the confined area. Begin rally from behind service line. Rotate the serve with each point.

4. In partners, play a half court singles game (11 points). Play a regular game except the service is straight ahead instead of diagonal.

5. In groups of four, play a doubles game with all shots taken either between the net and short service line or between the long service lines. After the serve, all shots falling within the service courts are out of bounds. Play an 11-point game.

6. View the loop film on "Round-the-Head Stroke" and read the skill analysis in one of the badminton books. In partners, A and B rally using clears and round-the-head strokes. Continue until each has hit 5 round-the-head clears and 5 round-the-head smashes.

7. Read the skill analysis for the drive serve in one of the badminton books. Explain and demonstrate the serve to your instructor.

8. In partners, A completes 10 drive serves while B tries to return. Reverse.

TASK SHEET — GAME PLAY

STUDENT _____

Tasks to be self checked and dated.

	SELF	DATE

1. Play 3 games of singles. Each game is to be against a different classmate.

   1.1 Person played _____
       Score _____

   1.2 Person Played _____
       Score _____

   1.3 Person Played _____
       Score _____

2. Play a set of singles out of class.
   Person Played _____
   Score _____

3. Play a game of mixed doubles using up and back formation.

   Team A _____ & _____
   Team B _____ & _____
   Score A _____ B _____

4. Play a game of mixed doubles using a side by side formation and a different partner.

   Team A _____ & _____
   Team B _____ & _____
   Score A _____ B _____

5. Play a game of mixed doubles using a combination or rotation formation and a different partner.

   Team A _____ & _____
   Team B _____ & _____
   Score A _____ B _____

6. Play 1 set of mixed doubles out of class.

   Team A _____ & _____
   Team B _____ & _____
   Score A _____ B _____

7. Play a game of doubles using the formation of your choice.

	SELF	DATE

Team A _____ & _____
Team B _____ & _____
Score A _____ B _____

8. Play a game of doubles with instructor as partner.

Team A _____ & Doe _____
Team B _____ & _____
Score A _____ B _____

9. Play a set of doubles out of class.

Team A _____ & _____
Team B _____ & _____
Score A _____ B _____

SUMMARY
1. _____ Number of tasks completed.
2. _____ Number of singles *games* won _____ lost _____ .
3. _____ Number of doubles *games* won _____ lost _____ .

Student _____

Loop Film Task Overhead Forehand Strokes — Clear

1. Draw racket face position showing contact for clear. (Side view)

2. What is the flight of the shuttle? Draw a dotted line starting with contact point at left side of the net to placement on the right side.

_____ | _____

3. Describe body position at contact.

    3.1 Hips

    3.2 Stance (base of support)

    3.3 Direction feet are facing

    3.4 Body weight

    3.5 Racket arm

Student _____

Loop Film Task Overhand Forehand Strokes — Drop

1. Draw racket face position showing contact for drop. (Side view)

2. What is the flight of the shuttle? Draw a dotted line starting with contact point at left side of the net to placement on the right side.

_____ | _____

3. Describe body position at contact.

    3.1 Hips

    3.2 Stance (base of support)

    3.3 Direction feet are facing

    3.4 Body weight

    3.5 Racket arm

Student _____

Loop Film Task Underhand Net Shots

1. For both forehand and backhand underhand net strokes, which leg is forward?

2. Compare the amount of force used in the underhand net strokes with the overhand strokes.

3. What is the racket face position on net strokes?

4. How high above the net should net strokes travel? What could happen if the flight is high?

_____

Student _____

1. In relation to the body, where should the shuttle be contacted for the drive?

2. What is the flight pattern of the drive in relation to the net?

SKILL ANALYSIS

Overhand Clear

PURPOSE: To send the shuttle high and deep into the opponent's court.

SKILL ANALYSIS:
1. Use a forehand grip for forehand clears and backhand grip for backhand clears.
   - 1.1   Forehand Grip
      - 1.1.1. Shake hands with the racket handle so that the butt of the handle rests against the base of the hand.
      - 1.1.2 Place the "V" formed by the thumb and forefinger over the top bevel of the handle.
      - 1.1.3 Spread the forefinger slightly apart in a trigger finger pose.
      - 1.1.4 Wrap the thumb naturally around the handle.
   - 1.2   Backhand Grip
      - 1.2.1 Rotate the racket one quarter turn clockwise so the "V" is over the top left bevel.
      - 1.2.2 Extend the thumb up along the back bevel of the handle.
2. Take a left forward stride position.
3. Drop racket low behind the back, wrist and arm cocked.
4. Lead with the elbow.
5. Rotate body quickly and transfer weight forward with the swing.
6. Contact shuttle slightly forward on the right side.
7. Angle racket face slightly upward on contact.
8. Follow through high and forward.

Serve

PURPOSE: To put the shuttle into play by sending the shuttle over the net and into the diagonal court with an underhand stroke.

SKILL ANALYSIS:
Rules:
1. Contact shuttle below waist height.
2. Keep racket head lower than hand on contact.
3. Maintain established foot position until shuttle is served.

Serve:
1. Use a forehand grip.
2. Take a left forward stride position in front court, knees flexed.
3. Hold the shuttle about chest high in front of right side.
4. Take the racket back about waist high, wrist cocked.
5. Release shuttle on forward swing.
6. Maintain cocked wrist on contact for short serve, uncock for deep serve.
7. Allow for minimal transfer of weight.

8. Contact shuttle ahead and away from body.
9. Adjust racket face angle for short and deep serves.
10. Follow through in direction of intended flight, a higher follow-through for deep serves.

Smash

PURPOSE: To produce a powerful, downward shot that is unreturnable.

SKILL ANALYSIS:
1. Take a left forward stride stance.
2. Drop racket head low behind back, wrist and arm cocked.
3. Lead with the elbow.
4. Extend racket arm fully.
5. Meet shuttle high and ahead of right foot.
6. Angle racket face downward on contact.
7. Transfer weight forward forcefully.
8. Snap the forearm and wrist.
9. Follow through in downward motion.

Overhand Drop

PURPOSE: To draw an opponent off guard by deceptively dropping the shuttle just over the net.

SKILL ANALYSIS:
1. Assume the same initiating mechanics for any other stroke.
2. Contact the shuttle farther ahead of the body than for the clear.
3. Angle the racket face slightly downward on contact.
4. Check the speed of the racket on contact.
5. Follow through gently in direction of intended flight.

Drive

PURPOSE: To draw an opponent off guard by deceptively dropping the shuttle just over the net.

SKILL ANALYSIS:
1. Assume a position with left shoulder toward the net and left foot forward.
2. Rotate body away from net for a long backswing.
3. Cock the wrist so racket head is above wrist level.
4. Transfer weight to forward foot on forward swing.
5. Contact shuttle in front of the left foot, about shoulder high and with flat racket head.
6. Extend the arm and uncock the wrist at contact.
7. Follow through parallel to floor and around left shoulder.

Underhand Net Shots

PURPOSE: To draw the opponent off guard by directing light, controlled shots from below net level so that the shuttle just clears the net and drops near the net.

SKILL ANALYSIS:
1. Grip loosely with spread fingers.
2. Use upper body for reaching instead of force production.
3. Bring racket back slightly from the wrist.
4. Contact shuttle well ahead of body.
5. Contact shuttle as close to net height as possible.
6. Stroke only with forearm, wrist, and hand.
7. Angle racket face according to desired placement.
8. Follow through slightly.

Section 2

Introduction to Activity Units

In the succeeding chapters, we have set forth twelve physical education activity units for which we have constructed numerous task learning experiences. The task learning experiences within each activity unit are subdivided according to individual skills. The activity units chosen by the authors are those most widely accepted and employed in an upper elementary, junior, and senior high school physical education curriculum. The Selected Fundamental Skills unit purposely precedes the other chapters because it deals with some of the basic body movements inherent in all other physical education activities and provides a foundation for sports and rhythms.

Each skill within the twelve activity units is characterized by three divisions: Purpose, Skill Analysis, and Task Learning Experiences. The Purpose sets the direction for which the skill will be utilized during the lesson and alerts the students to the skill objective. By examining the Purpose the student can clearly understand the intent in employing the skill. The teacher may choose to stress the Purpose by highlighting it on a chalkboard or bulletin board for student assimilation.

The Skills Analysis is likewise written in student terms in order to sequentially guide the student through the execution of the skill. Each phase of the performance of the skill is described simply and concisely for thorough understanding. Although it is designed for the student, the teacher can utilize the Skill Analysis as a review prior to a direct instructional approach or as a teaching aid for students needing remedial work in skill acquisition. The Skill Analysis might be copied on charts and placed on the walls for student references while each progresses through task learning experiences.

The Task Learning Experiences are the primary focus of the text. Although they are written in student terms, the teacher may choose to reword or rewrite the tasks in terms of familiar vocabulary or for a varied age level. The tasks are arranged progressively according to difficulty and practicality of utilization. However, as was alluded to in Chapter 2, the task learning experiences may be used in various ways other than sequentially. A complete overview of various means for utilizing task learning experiences was presented in the Organizing Strategies section of Chapter 2.

FIVE

Selected Fundamental Skills

ROTARY AND LINEAR MOTION

Purpose:
To demonstrate an understanding of linear and rotary motion and its applicability to body movement.

Skill Analysis: Definitions
1. Rotary motion is movement around an axis. All parts of an object move in a full circle.
2. Linear motion is the result of the whole body moving from point A to point B at a like rate of speed. Total object or body moves in the same direction, same distance, and same speed.
3. The combination of rotary and linear motion is the result of the whole body moving linearly while some body parts are generating rotary motion.

Task Learning Experiences:
1. Using a locomotor skill, move in the gym concentrating on recognizing all body parts moving in a rotary motion. Identify and count how many. Try at least five locomotor skills (run, skip, hop, etc.)
2. Repeat Task #1 utilizing locomotor skills in a variety of directions. Try at least four locomotor skills in at least four different directions.
3. Produce a linear movement in an up-and-down direction. Repeat five times.

4. Vary the extensions, produce a high jump followed by a low jump. Flow and an even rhythm are important. Repeat five times.
5. Using a jump rope, try a succession of jumps as the arms' rotary motion turns the rope. Think about the linear and rotary motion being used.
6. Alternate feet (bases of support) as you turn the rope. Try at least three different combinations of foot patterns; i.e., one foot, crossed feet, skipping.
7. Move while jumping rope and create different pathways (straight, circular, zig-zag, etc.), using lineary motion. Try at least three pathways.
8. Create a routine which includes three different pathways, three different directions, and three different locomotor skills.

THROW

Purpose:
To propel an object through space by imparting force to the object using either an overhand, underhand, or sidearm pattern.

Skill Analysis:
1. Use the following to increase speed and distance:
   1.1 Throw from a stable base.
   1.2 Transfer body momentum to the object.
   1.3 Utilize powerful sequential muscle groups.
   1.4 Increase the speed of body part movements.
   1.5 Shift the center of gravity from backward to forward.
   1.6 Increase the length of the lever.
   1.7 Stride in opposition.
   1.8 Precede the release with a step or two.
   1.9 Follow through.
2. Determine flight direction by the direction the hand is moving at the time of release and the direction of the follow-through motion of the hand and arm.
3. Include the following when throwing:
   3.1 Focus on the target.
   3.2 Stride with left foot forward.
   3.3 Rotate the throwing side away from the intended flight on backswing (less rotation for underhand throw).
   3.4 Take the throwing arm backward and upward (downward and backward for underhand throw).
   3.5 Cock the wrist at the end of the backswing.
   3.6 Rotate the throwing side forward and transfer the weight.
   3.7 Lead with the elbow except in the underhand throw.
   3.8 Release with a wrist snap.
   3.9 Follow through in the direction of intended flight.

Task Learning Experiences

1. Take a forward stride position (left foot forward) and throw a bean bag forward with an underarm motion five times. Repeat concentrating on taking the arm all the way back and rotating the body back with the arm swing. Repeat five times.
2. Repeat Task #1 concentrating on the release. Shift the weight forward and follow through. Repeat five times increasing the speed of all movement.
3. Repeat Tasks #1 and #2 throwing at a target. Arrange targets on a wall or floor and change distances and target sizes.
4. Repeat Tasks #1, #2, and #3 using various kinds of balls.
5. Repeat Tasks #1, #2, #3, and #4 using an overhand throw. Concentrate on taking the object back behind the shoulder and leading with the elbow.
6. Place a large ball on the floor and throw smaller balls at it trying to move the larger ball. Concentrate on forceful throws.
7. Repeat Task #6 adding several players to form two teams. Team A tries to move the ball across a designated area while Team B tries to move the ball across a designated area in the opposite direction. Use several throwing balls. Add rules and scoring.
8. From a sitting position, throw several balls and bean bags overhand for distance. What happens to the amount of force? Lie on the floor and throw the ball as high as possible. Is there more or less force?
9. Throw for distance from a standing position and then add two or three steps. Which gave more distance? Repeat another time.
10. Use a wall target and successfully hit the target five out of 10 times from 10 feet, 20 feet, 30 feet, and 40 feet.
11. Repeat Task #10 using different sized and weighted balls.
12. In partners, throw and catch using a bean bag. Complete 5 consecutive throws and catches without a miss. Complete 10. Repeat increasing the distance.
13. Repeat Task #12 using different sized and weighted balls.
14. Repeat Tasks #12 and #13 with both partners moving through space about 10-15 feet apart.
15. In partners, A throws to B who is moving forward, then laterally, and then diagonally. Complete five successful throws and catches. Reverse.
16. Play a modified game of softball with a batter standing on home plate and throwing a ball of choice from an assortment of sizes and shapes. The ball must travel a prescribed distance in the air. Add rules as needed.

CATCH

Purpose:
To absorb the force of an oncoming object by stopping and holding the object.

Skill Analysis:

1. Maintain body balance by using a forward-backward stride.
2. Keep the center of gravity over the base of the support.
3. Focus and track the oncoming object.
4. Align the body with the oncoming object.
5. Use a receiving surface that is as large as possible.
6. Position the hands in relationship to the size of the thrown object.
7. Bring the object as near to the center of gravity as possible.
8. Let the arms and hands "give" as the object contacts the hands.
9. Transfer weight back to help absorb the force of the caught object.

Task Learning Experiences:

NOTE: Complete Tasks #1-#14 in partners and reverse.

1. Catch a ball five times in a forward stride position with a large base of support.
2. Catch a ball five times allowing the center of gravity to shift from the front to back edge of the base of support as the ball is caught.
3. Catch a low ball five times with the knees slightly bent and a lower center of gravity.
4. Catch a ball five times by moving behind it so that you are aligned with the oncoming ball.
5. Catch a ball five times by holding the hands in comparable size to the oncoming ball.
6. Catch a ball five times and "give" with it while bringing it toward the center of gravity and while shifting the body weight backward just at the moment of contact.
7. Catch a high thrown ball with the fingers pointed upward. Successfully catch five balls. Repeat with a high bounced ball.
8. Catch a low thrown ball with the fingers pointed downward. Successfully catch five balls. Repeat with a low bounced ball.
9. Repeat Tasks #1 through #8 using a variety of balls of different sizes, weight, and texture.
10. Repeat Tasks #1 through #8 using different thrown objects such as a bean bag, medicine ball, deck tennis ring, frisbee, etc. Do the same basic principles apply to each object? (Exclude the bounce.)
11. Catch a thrown ball and immediately throw to your partner. Repeat five times.
12. Repeat Task #11 but throw to a moving partner.
13. Catch a thrown ball and immediately run forward. Repeat five times.
14. Repeat Task #13 running to the left, to the right, diagonally forward or turning and running in the opposite direction. Repeat each three times.

STRIKING

Purpose:
To propel an object through space by imparting a sudden force with an implement or body part.

Skill Analysis:
1. Focus eyes on the object to be hit.
2. Rotate body weight away from the object and then transfer weight to the object.
3. Follow through in the direction of the intended flight.

Principles:
1. A longer lever imparts more speed.
2. The speed and weight of the striking implement will affect the speed and/or the distance of the projected object.
3. Usually the greater the size and weight of the hit object, the less distance it travels.

Task Learning Experiences:
1. Place a soccer or playground ball on the floor or ground. From a stationary position kick the ball three times concentrating on backswing, contact, and follow through.
2. Repeat Task #1 concentrating on increasing the speed of the leg. Does the ball move faster and farther? Repeat three times.
3. Repeat Tasks #1 and #2 kicking the ball into a wall and kicking the rebound. Repeat taking one step before kicking. What are the results?
4. Place a softball or a 6″ playground ball on a batting tee and use a bat to hit the ball off the tee. Hit five balls. Concentrate on backswing, contact, and follow through. Repeat concentrating on rotating the weight back with the backswing and then forward on contact and follow through.
5. Repeat Task #4 by contacting the ball high, center, and low. How does this affect the flight?
7. Repeat Task #4 by substituting a wand for a wooden or aluminum bat. How does this affect the speed and distance of the ball?
8. In partners, repeat the striking concepts of Tasks #4, #5, and #6 without a tee. A throws to B who hits. Does the speed of a pitched ball contribute to hitting distance?
9. Using a beachball, throw it upward with one hand and hit it with the other hand. Alternate using underhand, sidearm, and overhand hits. Repeat each five times. Concentrate on rotating the weight back with the backswing and then forward on contact and follow through.
10. Repeat Task #9 from a sitting, squatting, and kneeling position. What are the results? In which position was more force produced? Less force?

11. Repeat Tasks #9 and #10 using a volleyball.
12. Repeat Task #9 by contacting the ball high or on top, center, and low or under. Use either a beachball or volleyball. What are the flight results?
13. Concentrate on accuracy by hitting either a volleyball or beach-ball into a marked wall target five out of ten times. Repeat increasing the distance from the target.
14. Arrange two hula hoops on the floor so that one is five to eight feet behind the other. Stand behind a line ten feet away and repeat Task #9 trying to place the ball so that it bounces inside one hoop and then the other. What adjustments are necessary for success? Repeat increasing the distance between the hoops. Repeat rearranging the hoops in different positions.
15. Hit a self-tossed shuttlecock or yarnball with the open palm of the hand five times. Repeat using a paddle, then a badminton racket. Which produced more speed, force, distance? Why?
16. From a batting tee, hit a tennis ball, softball, and soccer ball using a regular bat. Which object traveled the greatest distance? What might have caused this?

RUN

Purpose:
To move quickly by transferring the weight from one foot to another.

Skill Analysis:
1. Run on the balls of the feet.
2. Maintain a forward body lean.
3. Move arms and legs in opposition.
4. Lift the knees upward and forward in the direction of the run.

Task Learning Experiences:
1. Accelerate from a walk to a run by gradually increasing the force of the push against the floor. Note the sudden lack of double support or the addition of no support.
2. Run and concentrate upon receiving the body weight on the ball of the foot and pushing off as much as possible to increase speed.
3. Stand straight with the feet together and the arms down at the side. At a signal, break into a few running steps to a fast run. Try several times.
4. Repeat Task #3 starting with knees bent, a slight forward lean, and the arms up in opposition. Try several times.
5. Repeat Task #4 with a deep knee bend, one foot forward, hands on the floor, head (focus) forward, and center of gravity over front foot. Repeat five times.
6. Run and on signal stop. Plant one foot forward to absorb the transfer of the center of gravity. Try several times.

Keeping the center of gravity low aids in changing directions quickly

7. Combine Tasks #5 and #6 with a start-run-stop.
8. Run without the use of the arms. Run with the use of the arms in opposition and concentrate on producing speed. Note the difference.
9. Run 25 yards, turn and run back to the original point. Work on increasing the efficiency of the run.
10. Run varying the length of the stride. Try small steps, large steps, combinations. What do you find is true about an efficient run (combination of sizes)?
11. Run changing directions and pathways. Try as many pathways and direction combinations as you can.
12. Race someone, varying distances, and evaluate performances for efficiency.
13. Race against several students. Concentrate on efficient movement.

JUMP AND LAND

Purpose:
To propel one's body in a horizontal or vertical direction through the use of a one or two foot take off. The landing consists of absorbing the force with both feet in order to avoid injury.

Skill Analysis:

Jump
1. Bend the knees and waist initially in order to gain maximum force from the extension during the jump.
2. Swing the arms back and forth to gain momentum.
3. Lean the body forward to gain height.

Land
1. Land on the balls of the feet.
2. Bend the knees upon landing.
3. Place the feet shoulder width apart upon landing.
4. Focus the eyes ahead in order to maintain balance.

Task Learning Experiences:
1. Jump up (vertically), concentrating on landing on the balls of the feet and bending the knees to absorb shock.
2. Jump up (vertically), concentrating on landing with the feet approximately shoulder width apart in order to maintain balance.
3. Jump up (vertically) at a low level and then jump up (vertically) at a high level.
4. Jump up (vertically), gradually increasing the height from the lowest level to the highest level in seven jumps. Then decrease from the highest level to the lowest level in seven jumps.
5. Jump forward (horizontally) from a starting line five times. With each repetition attempt to increase the distance of the jump.
6. Take a few running steps and jump forward (horizontally), concentrating on form.
7. Repeat Task #6 jumping your maximum distance. This distance should be at least four feet.
8. Take a few running steps and jump forward (horizontally) attempting to land with feet together. You should be successful four out of five times.
9. Repeat Task #8 landing in a forward-backward stride position. Try five times maintaining balance.
10. Repeat Task #9 continuing with a run after the jump. Try five times.
11. Repeat Task #8 landing with knees and waist bent (squat) and with hands in front on the floor. Try five times attempting to increase the distance of the jump.
12. Jump over four objects of different heights in order to practice landing.

Jumping off an object

13. Jump off a box or ledge (two to three feet high) in order to practice landing.
14. Repeat Task #13 landing on one foot.
15. Repeat Task #13 making a half turn before landing.
16. Repeat Task #13 making a full turn before landing.

SIX

Badminton

OVERHAND CLEAR

Purpose:
To send the shuttle high and deep into the opponent's court.

Skill Analysis:
1. Use a forehand grip for forehand clears and a backhand grip for backhand clears.
    1.1. Forehand Grip
        1.1.1 Shake hands with the racket handle so that the butt of the handle rests against the base of the hand.
        1.1.2 Place the "V" formed by the thumb and forefinger over the top level of the handle.
        1.1.3 Spread the forefinger slightly apart in a trigger finger pose.
        1.1.4 Wrap the thumb naturally around the handle.
    1.2 Backhand Grip
        1.2.1 Rotate the racket one quarter turn clockwise so the "V" is over the top left bevel.
        1.2.2 Extend the thumb up along the back bevel of the handle.
2. Take a left forward stride position.
3. Drop racket low behind the back wrist and arm cocked.
4. Lead with the elbow.
5. Rotate body quickly and transfer weight forward with the swing.
6. Contact shuttle slightly forward on the right side.

7. Angle racket face slightly upward on contact.
8. Follow through high and forward.

Kinds: underhand, backhand

Task Learning Experiences:

1. In partners, A takes a forehand grip and B assesses the grip according to the skill analysis. Reverse.
2. Repeat Task #1 using a backhand grip.
3. Swing the racket for a clear 10 times. Concentrate on a forceful swing. Listen for a swishing sound.
4. Self toss a shuttle high and clear against a wall. Repeat 8-10 times from a distance of 10-15 feet. Concentrate on timing and force.
5. In partners, A tosses high shuttles to B who clears against a wall. Repeat 10 times clearing from a distance of 20 feet and reverse. Increase distance to 30 feet, 40 feet, depending on age, grade, and developmental level of pupil.
6. Repeat Task #5 and record number of hits against the wall out of 10 trials.
7. Repeat Tasks #4, #5 and #6 using an underhand clear.
8. Stand in the center of a court and self-toss the shuttle high and clear over the net to the back court area. Repeat 10 times.
9. Repeat Task #8 recording the number of clears that land between the back boundary lines.

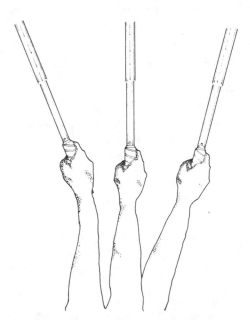

Racket contact for smash, drop, and clear

10. Repeat Task #8 jumping off the floor just prior to contacting the shuttle. Which position allowed for more force production, thus more distance?
11. Repeat Tasks #8 and #9 using an underhand clear.
12. In groups of three, A tosses the shuttle to B who clears over the head of A and C retrieves. Clear as far as possible. Toss five shuttles and rotate.
13. Repeat Task #12 using an underhand clear. A backhand clear.
14. In partners, A serves high and deep to B who clears to back area of court. Repeat 10 times and reverse.
15. Repeat Task #14 using a backhand clear.
16. In partners, A and B stand about 20 feet apart and rally using the overhand, backhand, and underhand clear. Continue by increasing the distance to 25, 30, 35, and 40 feet.
17. In partners, each stands between back boundary lines and clears. Rally five consecutive clears. Rally 10. Rally 15. Do not count if either must take more than one step into the court to clear.

SERVE

Purpose:
To put the shuttle into play by sending the shuttle over the net into the diagonal court with an underhand stroke.

Skill Analysis:
Rules
1. Contact shuttle below waist height.
2. Keep racket head lower than hand on contact.
3. Maintain established foot position until shuttle is served.

Serve
1. Use a forehand grip.
2. Take a left forward stride position in front court, knees flexed.
3. Hold the shuttle about chest high in front of right side.
4. Take the racket back about waist high, wrist cocked.
5. Release shuttle on forward swing.
6. Maintain cocked wrist on contact for short serve, uncock for deep serve.
7. Allow for minimal transfer of weight.
8. Contact shuttle ahead and away from body.
9. Adjust racket face angle for short and deep serves.
10. Follow through in direction of intended flight, a higher follow through for deep serves.

Kinds: Short and low, Long and deep, Driven

Task Learning Experiences:
1. Serve 10 shuttles against a wall concentrating on the timing of the drop and swing.
2. Repeat Task #1 concentrating on the mechanics and rules governing the serve.
3. Stand behind a line 6½ feet from a wall and serve above a 5-foot line on the wall. Serve 10 trials. Serve 10 consecutive good serves.
4. In partners, repeat Task #3 serving 10 shuttles between a five and seven-foot line on the wall.
5. Repeat Task #3 serving 10 shuttles between a five and seven-foot line on the wall.
6. Stand in the front inside corner area of a court without a net and serve 10 shuttles into a legal court diagonally across from your court.

7. Repeat Task #6 serving into the front one-third of the court.
8. Repeat Task #6 serving into the back one-third of the court.
9. Repeat Tasks #7 and #8 from a center court serving position. What kind of adjustments are necessary to produce differing amounts of force?
10. Repeat Tasks #6, #7 and # 8 with a net at legal height.
11. Repeat Tasks #6, #7 and #8 from an adjacent court.
12. Serve 10 shuttles short and low into different areas of the front singles court. Doubles court.
13. Serve 10 shuttles long and high into different areas of the back singles court. Doubles court.
14. Stretch a line two feet above and parallel to the top of the net. Serve 10 shuttles between the net and line and into the front court.
15. Repeat Task #14 moving the line to one foot above the net.
16. In partners, A serves to B who returns the serve. Serve five and reverse. Complete three trials.
17. Repeat Task #16 serving to different court areas. Discuss which service areas are the most difficult to return. Easiest?
18. In partners, A serves high to B who smashes the return. Serve a mixture of placements. Serve 10 and reverse. Discuss where the best areas are to avoid a smash return.
19. Repeat Task #16 adding a scoring element. Score one point for the server if the receiver fails to return the serve or a legal return. Score one point for the receiver if the server fails to complete a legal serve and when the receiver returns a serve legally. Continue until either scores 10 points.
20. In partners, A serves, B returns and A returns. Serve five times and reverse. Discuss serving strategies for best possible court position for hitting the returned serve. Check your discussion points by repeating serve, return, return.

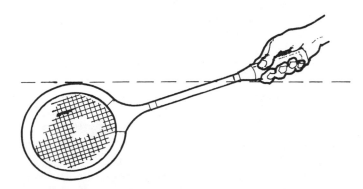

Relationship of hand and racket for legal serve

SMASH

Purpose:
To produce a powerful, downward shot that is unreturnable.

Skill Analysis:
1. Take a left forward stride stance.
2. Drop racket head low behind back, wrist and arm cocked.
3. Lead with the elbow.
4. Extend racket arm fully.
5. Meet shuttle high and ahead of right foot.
6. Angle racket face downward on contact.
7. Transfer weight forward forcefully.
8. Snap the forearm and wrist.
9. Follow through in downward motion.

Task Learning Experiences:
1. Stand 10 feet from a wall and self toss the shuttle high. Hit the shuttle against the bottom of the wall. Repeat 10 times.
2. Repeat Task #1 hitting at a target marked near the bottom of the wall. Score three out of ten, 5/10.
3. In partners, A tosses the shuttle high to B who tries to hit and direct it forcefully at A's feet. Reverse after 10 trials. Together discuss:
   3.1 In order to direct the shuttle at your partner's feet, where, in relation to the body, did you contact the shuttle?
   3.2 What was the angle of the racket face on contact?
   Now repeat two more trials of five shuttles each and note the above questions.
4. In partners, and on a court with a net, A tosses the shuttle high to racket side of B who smashes. Repeat 10 times and reverse.
5. Repeat Task #4 with A tossing high to non-racket side of B who uses a backhand smash.
6. In partners, A tosses the shuttle high to different areas of the court. Reverse and discuss:
   6.1 From what areas of the court were you most successful in smashing?
   6.2 How would you relate this to your opponent's chance of returning a smash?
7. Repeat Task #6 with A serving a high shuttle to B who smashes and A tries to return the smash. Repeat 10 times and reverse. Discuss again the questions in Task #6.
8. In partners, A serves high shuttles to B who smashes to various areas of the court. Repeat 10 times and reverse. Note the angle of the racket face at contact.
9. Repeat Task #8 placing five smashes down the right side of the court. Down the left side.

10. Repeat Task #8 with floor targets arranged on the court. Give point values for each. Record total score after 10 trials.
11. In partners, A serves the shuttle high to B who smashes to A's forehand side five times and to A's backhand five times. A tries to return each smash. Reverse. From which side was it more difficult to return the smash? Why?
12. In partners or groups of four, rally and use the smash whenever the shuttle is high and in the front half of the court.

DROP

Purpose:
To draw an opponent off guard by deceptively dropping the shuttle just over the net.

Skill Analysis:
1. Assume the same initiating mechanics for any other stroke.
2. Contact the shuttle farther ahead of the body than for the clear.
3. Angle the racket face slightly downward on contact.
4. Check the speed of the racket on contact.
5. Follow through gently in direction of intended flight.

Task Learning Experiences:
1. Self-toss the shuttle high and hit a drop shot concentrating on the point of contact and checking the swing. Repeat 10 times.
2. In partners, A tosses the shuttle high to B who assumes the same movement patterns as a clear but returns a drop shot. Toss 10 shuttles and reverse. Concentrate on reducing the speed of the racket and angling the racket face slightly downward on contact.
3. Repeat Task #1 from the front area of the court. Place 10 drop shots as close to the other side of the net as possible. Repeat from a center court position.
4. Repeat Task #2 on a court with A serving high shuttles to B who is hitting from the front area of the court. Try to place the shuttles as close to the other side of the net as possible. Repeat from a center court position.
5. Repeat Task #4 placing three out of ten between the net and service line. Placing 5/10. Placing 7/10.
6. Repeat Tasks #1-#5 using a backhand drop shot.
7. Repeat Task #3 from the back court position.
8. In partners, A serves high deep shuttles to B who is positioned in the back court. Try to place the shuttle as close to the other side of the net as possible. Reverse after returning five shuttles. Complete three trials.
9. Repeat Task #8 placing two out of five between the net and service line. Placing 3/5.

10. Repeat Tasks #7, #8 and #9 using a backhand drop shot.
11. In partners, rally mixing the drop and clear. Continue 4-5 minutes and concentrate on deceiving your opponent.
12. Repeat Task #11 adding the smash.

DRIVE

Purpose:
To execute a forceful sidearm stroke that will pass an opponent who is out of position.

Skill Analysis:
1. Assume a position with left shoulder toward the net and left foot forward.
2. Rotate body away from net for a long backswing.
3. Cock the wrist so racket head is above wrist level.
4. Transfer weight to forward foot on forward swing.
5. Contact shuttle in front of the left foot, about shoulder high with a flat racket head.
6. Extend the arm and uncock the wrist at contact.
7. Follow through parallel to floor and around left shoulder.

Task Learning Experiences:
1. Swing the racket five times using a forehand drive. Concentrate on the mechanics of the swing. Listen for a swishing sound. Repeat using a backhand drive.
2. Stand about 10 feet from a wall and self-toss a shuttle. Hit using a forehand drive. Repeat 10 times. Concentrate on producing a forceful drive and keeping the shuttle flight parallel to the floor.
3. Repeat Task #2 directing the flight as close as possible to a line five feet high.
4. Repeat Tasks #2 and #3 using a backhand drive.
5. In partners, A and B rally from center court positions using forehand drives. Concentrate on powerful strokes and maintaining a parallel-to-the-floor flight pattern.
6. Repeat Task #5 using backhand drives.
7. Repeat Tasks #5 and #6 with A and B in opposite diagonal courts so that all hits are crosscourt drives.
8. In groups of four, each assumes a center court position. Rally using the forehand and backhand drive. Concentrate on placing the drives either crosscourt or down the line.
9. In groups of four, A and C take a position between the net and the service line. B and D remain in center court positions and rally using the drive. A and C try to block the drive and direct the shuttle downward toward an open space. After 4-5 minutes, rotate positions.
10. Repeat Task #9 adding a scoring method.

11. In partners, rally by combining a mixture of strokes with the drive.
12. Repeat Task #11 in groups of four.

UNDERHAND NET SHOTS

Purpose:
To draw the opponent off guard by directing light, controlled shots from below net level so that the shuttle just clears the net and drops near the net.

Skill analysis:
1. Grip loosely with spread fingers.
2. Use upper body for reaching instead of force production.
3. Bring racket back slightly from the wrist.
4. Contact shuttle well ahead of body.
5. Contact shuttle as close to net height as possible.
6. Stroke only with forearm, wrist and hand.
7. Angle racket face according to desired placement.
8. Follow through slightly.

Task Learning Experiences:
1. Mark two parallel lines, five feet and six feet on a wall. Stand with left shoulder toward the wall and about 3-4 feet from it. Self drop shuttles from above the five foot line. Guide and direct the shuttle between the lines and *gently* against the wall. If the shuttle rebounds more than two feet from the wall, reduce the force of the swing.
2. Repeat Task #1 recording the number of good hits. Do not count rebounds of more than two feet.
3. Repeat Task #1 scoring five consecutive hits.
4. Repeat Tasks #2 and #3 by standing and facing the wall.
5. Repeat Tasks #1, #2 and #3 by standing with the right shoulder to the wall. Toss shuttle instead of dropping it.

Position of racket for underhand net shot

6. In partners and on court, A tosses shuttles just over the net and in front of the service line to B's forehand side. B returns with an underhand net shot. Concentrate on returning close to the top of the net and in front of the service line. Repeat five times and reverse. Complete three trials.
7. Repeat Task #6 until each partner is successful five times.
8. Repeat Tasks #6 and #7 tossing the backhand side.
9. Repeat Tasks #6 and #7 with both A and B hitting and returning net shots.
10. Repeat Task #9 concentrating on angled flight patterns mixing straight up and down shots with cross court shots.
11. Stretch a rope 18 inches above and parallel to the top of the net. In partners, A and B assume a position between the net and the service line on opposite sides. Rally net shots for three minutes and count the number of placements between the rope and net that qualify as net shots.
12. Using the same apparatus and positions in Task #11 score a point each time a net shot is not legally returned provided the net shot went between the net and rope and dropped between the net and the service line. Continue for three minutes.
13. In partners, A serves short and low to B who returns a net shot. Serve five and reverse. Continue for five trials.
14. Rally for five minutes and use a net shot whenever appropriate.

SEVEN

Basketball

PASS

Purpose:
To move the ball between at least two players and to maintain possession while maneuvering into goal-shooting position.

Skill Analysis:
Basic to All Passing
1. Hold ball with fingertips.
2. Release ball with wrist and finger snap.
3. Extend arms and fingers in direction of the pass.
4. Step in direction of the pass.
5. Pass to receiver's chest area.
6. Pass ahead of moving teammates.
7. Avoid long cross-court passes — short, quick passes are more effective.
8. Use fake passes and eye deception.
9. See Selected Fundamental Skills for throwing and catching.

   Kinds: chest, bounce, baseball, overhead, underhand, and hook.

Additional Skill Analyses:
Chest Pass
1. Use two hands on the ball at chest level.
2. Place the thumbs behind the ball and fingers extending upward and slightly forward.

3. Keep the elbows flexed and close to body.
4. Push the arms forward.
5. Give an extra push with the thumbs on release.

Two Hand Bounce Pass
1. Use basic analysis of chest pass.
2. Begin the pass at waist level rather than chest.
3. Push downward to a spot on the floor.
4. Remember that the angle of rebound is an important factor.

One Hand Bounce Pass
1. Begin the pass between the shoulders and waist.
2. Balance the ball with the nonpassing hand.
3. Place the passing hand behind and toward top of ball with fingers extending upward.
4. Keep the passing elbow flexed and close to the body.
5. See Skills #3 and #4 under two hand bounce pass.

Baseball Pass
1. Begin the pass behind the shoulder about ear level.
2. Place the passing hand under and behind the ball.
3. Cock the wrist.
4. Keep the elbow flexed and away from the body.

Overhead Pass
1. Begin the pass above the head.
2. Place the fingers on the side and rear of the ball extending upward.
3. Place the thumbs under the ball.
4. Flex the elbows and wrists slightly.
5. Release the ball in front of the body about head level.
6. Follow through with the hands to eye level.

Two Hand Underhand Pass
1. Begin the pass from the front of the body (abdomen) or from either hip.
2. Place the fingers on the side and rear of ball extending downward.
3. Place the thumbs on top of the ball.
4. Flex the elbows and point away from the body.

Hook Pass
1. Begin the pass from an extended arm position to the side.
2. Place the hand under the ball—palm up.
3. Align the nonpassing shoulder with the receiver.
4. Raise the passing arm sideward so it crosses the passing shoulder and over the head.
5. Release the ball from an extended body or jump position.

The hook pass

6. Direct the ball downward.
7. Follow through with the palm facing downward.

Task Learning Experiences:
1. In partners (using basketballs, soccer balls, volleyballs, or play balls) A and B execute 20 chest passes at a distance of 10 feet. Concentrate on mechanics. Repeat increasing distance.
2. Repeat Task #1 successfully completing 10, 15, 20 consecutive passes.
3. Repeat Tasks #1 and #2 using different passes.
4. Repeat Task #1 combining a reverse pivot and chest pass. A stands with back to B, pivots and passes to B. Reverse. Add side pivots and reverse turn.
5. Repeat Task #4 using a two hand bounce pass.
6. Using a wall, two balls, and from a distance of 12-15 feet, pass against the wall keeping two balls in play at once. Use one and two hand passes.
7. Using a wall target (hula hoop taped to wall) and from a marked-off distance, execute different passes in units of 10, 15, 20 for a specified time period aiming at the target.
8. For one and two handed bounce passes, practice against a wall target aiming for marked floor targets arranged so that the angle of rebound is varied. Study the results and determine best floor placement for the targets.

9. In groups of four, A, B, and C stand side by side and D faces them from a distance of 10 feet. D looks directly at B while passing to A and C who take a step laterally away from B after each pass. The object is to force peripheral vision. Rotate positions. Add a second ball.

10. In partners, A and B continue to execute chest passes while moving in different pathways through space. The whole class can be involved. This task is restricted by two rules. One, the player cannot walk while holding the ball, and two, players are not allowed to touch or bump. Stress body control and peripheral vision. Repeat using other passes.

11. In partners, walk and chest pass moving down the floor five times. Repeat moving at half speed. Repeat moving at full speed. Stress the rule of traveling.

12. Repeat Task #11 using different passes.

13. Combine passing with dribbling. In partners, A dribbles toward B and executes a chest pass. B repeats. Use different passes.

14. In small groups of four, passer stands at the top of the free throw lane with back to the basket and hook passes to teammates as they cut toward the basket from a diagonal side position. Receiver shoots. Concentrate on hitting the receiver at chest level and in front so the receiver does not break stride. Rotate positions after successfully passing five to ten balls.

15. In groups of three, A and B pass back and forth with C playing a defensive position. C moves to different positions between A and B. Is it easier to pass successfully when the defensive player is closer to the passer or farther away?

16. In groups of three, practice different passes using a defensive player. Play Keep Away with all moving. Rotate positions. Make up a scoring procedure.

17. Repeat Task #16 combining the pass with the dribble and other maneuvering tactics (pivoting, faking, feinting, and cutting).

18. Repeat Tasks #16 and #17 adding another defensive player.

19. Repeat Task #18 in groups of six with three offensive and three defensive players.

20. Repeat Task #19 adding goal shooting. Set a minimum of three, four, or five consecutive passes before allowing an attempt for goal.

DRIBBLE

Purpose:
To advance the ball through space by imparting force to the ball causing it to rebound off the floor while controlling and maintaining possession.

Skill Analysis:
1. Impart force downward with fingertips and wrist action.
2. Spread fingers for more control.
3. Flex knees.
4. Crouch body slightly.
5. Keep eyes alert to play situation.

Kinds: A close or loose dribble is determined by the angle of the directed force.

Task Learning Experiences:
1. While sitting on a chair or bleacher seat, dribble the ball without looking at it. Change hands. Dribble from side to side using the same hand. Change hands. Repeat without looking at the ball.
2. In partners, repeat Task #1. A sits and dribbles while B stands in front of A and holds fingers up for A to count. The object is to keep the head up and eyes off the ball.
3. Dribble forward right-handed the width of the gym. Repeat five times.

4. Dribble forward left-handed the width of the gym. Repeat five times.
5. Dribble forward alternating hands the width of the gym. Repeat five times.
6. Repeat Tasks #3, #4 and #5 moving backwards.
7. Repeat Tasks #3 and #4 moving sideways.
8. Repeat Tasks #3, #4 and #5 moving in a zigzag pathway.
9. Repeat Tasks #3, #4 and #5 moving in a circular pathway.
10. Repeat Tasks #3, #4 and #5 moving through an obstacle course.
11. Repeat Task #10 timed by a partner.
12. Dribble for endurance running at ½ or ¾ speed.
13. Dribble for endurance. Set a goal of three, five, or eight minutes.
14. Dribble and stop on signal command.
15. Dribble and change directions on signal command.
16. In partners, A dribbles in a stationary position and one hand bounce passes from the dribble to B who repeats. Try to make the movement continuous by letting the hand ride up with the ball and then push the ball. Repeat 10 times concentrating on making the movement fluid and angling the rebound to the partner's waist.
17. Repeat Task #16 while moving side by side down court. Try with one partner on each side.
18. Repeat Tasks #16 and #17 using a one hand underhand pass.
19. In partners or small groups, dribble and pass down court.
20. Dribble and shoot using different shots.
21. One-on-One. In partners, stand in stationary position. Stand about two feet apart and face to face. A dribbles while B tries to deflect or steal the ball. Dribble high/low, fast/slow, eyes on ball/eyes on opponent, finger tip striking/whole palm striking. Do not make body contact. Reverse. Discuss what you discovered about ball control.
22. One-on-One. In partners, move through space. A dribbles the ball through space while B tries to deflect or steal the ball. Dribble close/loose, fast/slow, high/medium/low, straight pathway/zigzag, forward/sideward. Do not make body contact. Discuss what you discovered about maintaining ball possession and control.
    22.1 Is it easier for the defense to take away a close or loose dribble? Why?
    22.2 Is it easier for the defense to take away a fast or slow dribble? Why?
    22.3 What is the best height for dribbling if you are guarded? Why?
    22.4 How can you use your body to help maintain possession of the ball?
23. Continue One-on-One dribbling. Apply what you learned as a result of Task #21 and 22.

GOAL SHOOTING

Purpose:
To score points by sending the ball through the goal (basket).

Skill Analysis: Two Hand Chest Shot or Set Shot
1. Use the finger position of the chest pass.
2. Distribute the weight evenly.
3. Focus the eyes on rim of the basket.
4. Flex the knees and cock the wrists.
5. Extend arms upward and body follows.
6. Release with wrists straightening and fingers directing ball in upward arc.
7. Follow through with palms facing basket.

One Hand Set or Push Shot
1. Distribute the weight evenly over the balls of the feet.
2. Place the right foot slightly ahead.
3. Hold the ball about level with the right shoulder.
4. Place the left hand under and to left of the ball.
5. Place right hand behind and slightly under the ball with a cocked wrist.
6. Lower the ball and body slightly while focusing on the goal.

7. Extend the body upward and push the ball upward.
8. Release with a gentle wrist snap.
9. Follow through in direction of intended flight.

Jump Shot

1. Square the body toward basket.
2. Place left hand on side of ball for balance.
3. Place right hand behind ball.
4. Jump upward focusing the eyes on the basket.
5. Bring ball slightly above and in front of head.
6. Cock wrist and point elbow toward basket.
7. Follow through in direction of basket.

Two Hand Overhead Shot

1. Stand with body erect, head up and eyes on the target.
2. Flex the knees slightly.
3. Place thumbs under the ball with fingers on side and pointing upward and back.
4. Raise the ball overhead.
5. Swing the ball forward and upward.
6. Extend the arms and knees as the body weight shifts forward.

The jump shot

Lay-up Shot
1. Carry the ball with the left hand in front and under ball.
2. Place right hand on top and slightly behind.
3. Carry the ball to shoulder and head height as the left foot pushes off.
4. Lift the body with the right knee.
5. Direct the ball to the backboard with right hand.
6. Place the ball rather than throw against backboard.
7. Follow through with the palm of the right hand high in direction of backboard.

Hook Shot
1. Start with the back to the basket.
2. Place the right hand under the ball.
3. Extend the right arm away from the body.
4. Step with the left foot and turn toward the basket.
5. Bring the right arm upward to an overhead arc.
6. Release at the height of the extended arm with a wrist snap.
7. Follow through in direction of the basket.

Task Learning Experiences:
1. Use a two hand chest shot and shoot the ball 10 times toward a wall target 10-12 feet high from a distance of 6-8 feet. Arch the shot.
2. In partners, A holds a hula hoop at a high level. B uses a two hand chest shot and shoots the ball through the hoop 5-10 consecutive times from a distance of 6-8 feet. Reverse. Repeat from a longer distance and from different angles.
3. Stand close to the basket and shoot 10 balls using a two hand chest shot.
4. Standing close and using a two hand chest shot, try to make five baskets using the backboards and five without touching the rim or backboard.
5. From designated floor markings shoot 5-10 balls using a two hand chest shot.
6. Repeat Task #5 making two out of five, 3/5, or 4/5 goals.
7. In partners, A stands two feet away from B in a stationary guarding position while B attempts to make two out of 5, 3/5, or 4/5 goals.
8. Repeat Tasks #1-#7 using a push shot, jump shot, and two handed overhead shot.
9. Dribble to a floor spot and shoot using a push shot, jump shot, and two hand chest shot. Concentrate on smooth transition from dribble to shooting.
10. In partners, A drives (dribbles) to a floor spot where B has moved in to guard. A executes a jump shot. Repeat five times and reverse. Use different shots.

11. Repeat Task #10 in a one-on-one play. After each basket, the other partner starts the play from out court.
12. From designated floor markings around the key area, shoot five hook shots.
13. Repeat Task #12 but fake right, hook left. Repeat five times.
14. Repeat Task #12 but fake right, dribble and hook left. Repeat five times.
15. Repeat Tasks #13 and #14 adding a defensive person. Reverse.
16. Repeat Task #15 making two out of five or three out of five goals.

Lay-Up Shot
17. Standing to the right side of the basket and within two feet, push the ball against the backboard until the ball successfully rebounds into the basket five out of 10 times. Concentrate on locating the spot on the backboard for banking the shot into the basket.
18. From a distance of 5-8 feet stride left and leap off the left foot bringing the right knee up as the ball is pushed by the right hand toward the spot which will bank the shot into the basket.
19. Repeat Task #18 combining a single dribble with the leap and shot. Begin about 10-12 feet away. Repeat five times.
20. Dribble from the right side at half speed concentrating on the mechanics of the lay-up and the spot on the backboard. Repeat the lay-up five times.

21. Repeat Task #20 increasing to normal speed.
22. Repeat Task #21 trying to complete two out of five, 3/5, or 4/5 goals.
23. Repeat Tasks #17-#22 from the left side of the basket.
24. Repeat Tasks #18-#22 down center by laying the ball over the rim rather than by banking the lay-up against the backboard.
25. In partners, A tries to make as many lay-ups as possible in 60 seconds. A starts from the free throw line, dribbles, executes the lay-up, retrieves the ball, and runs back across free throw line. B times and counts. Reverse.
26. Repeat Task #25 down center, left side, and alternating sides.
27. Make five, ten or fifteen consecutive goals using the lay-up shot.
28. In partners, combine the pass and lay-up moving side by side down court. Use one, two or three passes followed by a lay-up. Distance will depend on the number of passes.

Combine Faking and Shooting
29. Fake right and shoot (jump shot). Repeat five times.
30. Repeat Task #29 faking left.
31. Fake right, fake shot and drive right for a lay-up. Repeat five times.
32. Repeat Task #31 driving left for a lay-up.
33. Fake left, fake shot and drive right for a lay-up. Repeat five times.
34. Repeat Task #33 driving left for a lay-up.
35. In partners, A combines faking and shooting against B who acts as defensive player. After 10 attempts, reverse.

Foul Shots
36. Select a favorite free throw shooting style (two hand underhand, one hand set, or two hand set shot) and stand halfway between the free throw line and the basket. Successfully make three out of ten, 5/10 or 7/10 goals.
37. Repeat Task #36 moving back toward the free throw line.
38. Repeat Task #36 from the free throw line.

JUMP

Purpose:
To gain ball possession or direct the ball to a teammate or into the goal on rebounds, jump balls, and tipping.

Skill Analysis:
1. Jump from one or both feet.
2. Produce force by:
    2.1 Flexing the knees.
    2.2 Pushing off from the toes.
    2.3 Arching the back.
    2.4 Extending the body from toes to finger tips.

3. Absorb force by:
   3.1 Landing on the balls of the feet.
   3.2 Flexing ankles and knees.
4. Focus eyes on the ball at all times.
5. Remember that a player can reach about six inches higher if the player uses one hand instead of two.

Task Learning Experiences:
1. Run and on a signal, vertical jump as high as possible. Can be done in partners, small or large groups with either a student or teacher giving the signal.
2. Run to a marked spot on the floor. Jump into the air as high as possible and try to land on the same marked spot. Repeat five times.
3. From a crouch position, spring to a jump 10 times.
4. From a crouch position sideways to a wall, spring and jump. Touch the wall. Try to out jump your mark on each try.
5. Bounce the ball off the wall and jump to recover it. Try to recover the ball as high as possible. Vary the angles. Repeat 10 times.
6. Repeat Task #5 with a partner. A throws the ball at the wall while B recovers. Reverse.
7. Repeat Task #6 with a partner. After B jumps and recovers the ball, B passes to A. Reverse.
8. Repeat Task #5 but recover and dribble away. Repeat 10 times.
9. Bounce the ball off the wall and jump to tip the ball away. Tip as high as possible. Repeat 10 times.
10. In partners, repeat Task #7 but tip to partner.
11. In partners or small groups, bounce the ball off the backboard and each tries to tip the ball into the basket. Repeat until each has had five attempts.
12. Repeat Task #11 in groups of four or six. Half play defense and the other half offense. Defense tries to tip the ball away and the offense tries to tip the ball into the basket.
13. In groups of three, A tosses the ball for a center jump to B and C. Repeat five times and rotate positions. Vary partner heights for extra challenge.

GUARDING

Purpose:
To prevent the opponents from scoring, passing, receiving, and moving in accordance with basketball rules and to get possession of the ball.

Skill Analysis:
1. Take a wide forward stride position.
2. Keep weight forward over the balls of the feet but more over the forward foot.

3. Flex the ankles, knees, and hips for a low position.
4. Maintain an upright position if close to the goal.
5. Keep the head erect.
6. Use a windmill arm and hand position with one hand high to defend against the shot and one low to guard against the pass. To guard against a dribbler, keep both hands low.
7. Maintain a defensive position between the opponent and the goal.
8. Focus the eyes on the opponent's abdomen. (Less chance for being faked out).

Task Learning Experiences:

1. In a crouch position and the head up, roll a ball while sliding sideways, diagonally forward and backward. This will stress keeping the body low.
2. Assume windmill guarding position and slide to the right, left, forward, backward, diagonally forward left, right, and diagonally backward left, right. Keep the weight low and on the balls of the feet.
3. Repeat Task #2 with a leader calling directions or using hand signals.
4. In partners, A assumes defensive position facing B. A leader gives hand signals and B moves according to hand signal. A tries to move with B and maintain a position between B and the leader. Reverse. This can be a whole class or group drill.
5. In partners, A dribbles in place while B attempts to tap the ball away. Reverse.
6. In partners, A dribbles forward down the floor while B faces A and moves backwards in a guarding position. B concentrates on moving backwards, avoiding body contact, watching the dribble and timing. Reverse and repeat three times.
7. Repeat Task #6 adding ball deflection. B gets only one chance to deflect the ball within a prescribed distance. Reverse and repeat 3-5 times.
8. In partners, A dribbles toward B who moves in and tries to force A to the side line without body contact. Repeat five times. Reverse.
9. In partners, A fakes, drives and shoots while B concentrates on defending the play. Repeat five times. Reverse.
10. In partners, A shoots for goal from 10-18 feet away from the basket. B guards loosely from 2-3 feet away from A. As soon as A shoots, both quickly move toward the basket for the rebound. B concentrates on staying between A and the basket and tries to recover the rebound. Repeat five times. Reverse.
11. In groups of four, six, eight, or ten, play Keep Away using a player-to-player defense. Concentrate on guarding your opponent by playing the ball carrier and potential receiver closely. Exert constant pressure in hopes of forcing bad passes.
12. Repeat Task #11 adding goal shooting.

13. In two teams of three, four, or five each, Team A is assigned defense and sets a zone defense around the basket area. Defensive players guard any offensive player who comes into their area. Concentrate on shifting as a defensive unit in the zone area as play shifts from side to center to side. Continue play until a goal is scored or a defensive player gets the ball. Repeat five times. Reverse team.

EIGHT

Flag Football

PASS

Purpose:
To gain offensive yardage and to score.

Skill Analysis:
1. Grip the football so that the ring finger is over the second cross lace (for larger hands use the middle finger).
2. Rotate the body weight back with the carry using the nonthrowing hand to help guide the ball back.
3. Carry the ball back high and release high (above the head and away from the body).
4. Extend the nonthrowing hand out for counterbalancing just before the beginning of the pass.
5. Lead with the elbow.
6. Snap the wrist and fingers forward and outward on the release.
7. Transfer the body weight forward to the opposite foot.
8. Follow through in the direction of the intended flight.

Task Learning Experiences:
1. In partners, pass the ball back and forth concentrating on the mechanics of passing, control, and producing a spiral motion.
2. Repeat Task #1 increasing the distance. Concentrate on producing additional force.
3. In partners, A passes to B who is moving away from A in a forward direction. Repeat until successful three out of five times. Reverse.

4. Repeat Task #3 with B moving a few strides forward and then cutting to the left for a pass. Markers could be used to designate distances and cutting patterns. Repeat until successful three out of five times.
5. Repeat Task #4 with B cutting to the right. Mix pass patterns; slant, curl out and in, curl and go, etc.
6. Repeat Task #3 so that A is moving laterally while passing to B.
7. Pass the football at or through a stationary target (hoops attached to a strung rope or other suitable objects) five times. Repeat from different distances, angles, and after a step or two backwards or laterally.
8. Repeat Task #7 in small groups and add a scoring procedure.
9. In partners, A throws a large playground ball vertically into the air. B passes the football attempting to hit the ball. Reverse. Continue until successful two out of five times or three out of five times.
10. Repeat Task #9 in small groups and add a scoring procedure.
11. In groups of three, A and B take line positions. A centers to C who takes two or three steps backwards and passes to B who has moved down field. Repeat three times and rotate.
12. Repeat Task #11 with B moving straight ahead and cutting to the left. Cutting to the right.
13. Repeat Task #11 with B moving diagonally forward.
14. Repeat Tasks #3, #4, and #5 with a defensive player trying to deflect the ball. No body contact allowed.
15. Repeat Tasks #11 and #12 with a defensive player trying to deflect the ball. No body contact allowed.
16. Repeat Tasks #11 and #12 in fours with D added to the line position so that B and D are running down field as receivers. Pass to either.
17. In groups of six, repeat Task #16 against two defensive players. Scoring can be added. Choose pass plays to out maneuver the defense. Rotate positions.

CATCH

Purpose:
To maintain possession of the ball, advance in yardage, and score.

Skill Analysis:
1. Focus eyes on the oncoming ball.
2. Position hands together making certain to:
   2.1 Point little fingers together and downward for low balls — upward for high balls.

2.2 Place thumbs together and point fingers upward for balls coming directly at or above the receiver.
3. Give with hands and arms as the ball is caught.
4. Tuck the caught ball quickly into the body for carrying by:
    4.1 Gripping the end tightly.
    4.2 Placing the forearm on the outside of the ball.
    4.3 Forcing the other end of the ball toward the armpit.
5. Carry the ball in the arm away from the opponent.

Task Learning Experiences:

1. Toss the football up and catch it several times.
2. Toss the football up so that it will fall within 10 feet. Move to catch the ball. Repeat until successful 10 times.
3. Repeat Task #2 so that the catch is made while running and continue running a few strides.
4. Repeat Task #3 by faking, striding, and cutting after the catch and switching the ball from one carrying side to the other.
5. In partners, A and B pass back and forth concentrating on the mechanics of catching or receiving. Keep the fingers and arms relaxed at contact. Practice three to five minutes.
6. Repeat Task #5 concentrating on moving the ball immediately to a carrying position. Repeat until it becomes smooth and automatic.
7. Repeat Task # 6 passing and receiving with the receiver taking three or four quick strides as the ball is moved to the carrying position. Repeat until successful several times.
8. In partners, continue to pass and receive. A passes a few feet to the left or right of B who is running at half-speed. B catches the ball, and continues to move a few strides. Repeat until each is successful 10 times.
9. Repeat Task #8 changing the ball from one carrying arm position to the other.
10. Repeat Task #8 with the receiver faking one direction and moving in another after the catch.
11. Repeat Task #8 at a faster speed. After several successful receptions, add faking, changing directions, and switching the ball from arm to arm.
12. In threes, repeat Task #11 so that C is a defensive player who tries to tip or deflect the ball away. Repeat five times and rotate. Add a scoring element for more interest.
13. In partners, A kicks or punts the ball toward B who moves under the ball, catches it, and continues to run toward A. Complete five successful catches. Reverse.
14. Repeat Task #13 adding faking, cutting, and switching the carrying arm.

CENTERING

Purpose:
To put the ball into play.

Skill Analysis:
1. Assume a four-point position with the feet spread shoulder-width apart, knees flexed and weight evenly distributed over the balls of the feet.
2. Place the ball on the ground ahead of the shoulders.
3. Grip the ball with the right hand so that the fingers are on the laces toward the front end. The right hand snaps the ball.
4. Position the left hand on the opposite lower half of the ball. The left hand guides the ball.
5. Execute the following on a T-formation center.
   5.1 Keep the head up.
   5.2 Focus the eyes down field.
   5.3 Snap the ball up to the quarterback.
   5.4 Turn the ball a quarter turn to the left on the snap.
6. Execute the following on a set back or punt center.
   6.1 Keep the head down.
   6.2 Focus between the legs on intended receiver.
   6.3 Pass the ball back in a spiral.
   6.4 Direct the ball toward the waist of the receiver.

Task Learning Experiences:
1. In partners, A assumes a centering position for a set back hike and B evaluates the position according to the skill analysis. Reverse.
2. In partners, A centers to B who is three yards behind for receiving. Center five balls and reverse.
3. Repeat Task #2 until five successful receptions are completed. Reverse.
4. Repeat Tasks #2 and #3 increasing the distance to seven yards.
6. Center the ball to a set back so that the ball is directed about twelve inches to the left or right of the receiver depending on the predetermined side that the play will go. Complete five hikes to each side and reverse.
7. Practice the center by hiking the ball at a wall target from various distances. Try to hit the target three out of five times before changing the distance. Hoops could also be used as ground or floor targets.
8. In partners, A centers the ball and immediately moves faking a blocking maneuver while B quickly takes a few strides toward an imaginary goal. Repeat three times and reverse.
9. In threes, A centers to B who receives and passes to C who is moving down field. Repeat five times and rotate.

Centering the football

10. Repeat Task #9 with C running different patterns: curl out and in, flag, post, slant, curl and go, etc. Rotate positions.
11. In partners, A assumes a centering position for a T-formation hike. B evaluates the position according to the skill analysis. Reverse.
12. In partners, A hikes the ball into B's left hand while B is behind A with the hands under the center's crotch. B's fingers of the left hand are spread apart and the thumb is down. The right hand is above the left with the fingers pointing downward and the thumb close to the left thumb. Repeat five times or until a smooth snap is obtained. Reverse.
13. Repeat Task #8 with B fading back a few steps in pass position. A fakes a protective block. Reverse.
14. Repeat Task #9 using a T-formation hike.
15. Repeat Task #10 using a T-formation hike.

DEFLAG (TACKLE)

Purpose:
To deflag the ball carrier and stop the offensive play.

Skill Analysis:
1. Keep the weight low to facilitate quick movements.
2. Maintain a balanced position.

3. Use short, quick steps when moving to tackle.
4. Focus the eyes on the midsection of the ball carrier until ready to tackle—then shift eyes to flag.
5. Keep the arms and hands loose until they reach for the flag.

Task Learning Experiences:

1. In partners, face each other and move through space. Each partner tries to get the seat of the other as often as possible without touching other body parts. Count the number of tags. No holding is allowed. Set a three-minute time period.
2. Repeat Task #1 wearing flags. Attempt to deflag partner before being deflagged. Continue until one partner is successful five times.
3. Repeat Task #2 in small groups of five or six players. Each player acts as an independent and each tries to deflag the other players. Players are eliminated after being deflagged. Emphasize quick, deceptive movements.
4. In partners, establish two parallel goal lines about 20 feet apart. A carries the ball toward the opposite goal while B attempts to deflag. A scores a point if successful in reaching the goal without being deflagged. B scores a point if B legally deflags A. Reverse.
5. Repeat Task #4 in small opposing teams of two players.
6. In two teams of two each, Team A hikes the ball and runs a play.

Three-on-three flag football play

Team B starts from a three- or four-point stance and after the hike attempts to deflag team A. Repeat and rotate positions and rotate offense and defense.

7. Repeat Task # 6 by adding more players and using both running and passing plays.
8. In two teams of four players each, devise a play where the offensive team will center and pass or center and run for yardage. The defensive team will attempt to deflag the ball carrier or deflect the pass. Allow three plays per team before changing from offense to defense. Rotate positions within the team.
9. Repeat Task #8 by adding more rules and scoring.

KICK

Purpose:
To put the ball in play at the start of the half. Where goal posts are available, the kick is used to score a field goal and a point after touchdown.

Skill analysis:
For a held or teed ball
1. Flex the kicking leg at the knee and straighten as the ball is contacted by the toes.
2. Focus the eyes just below the midpoint of the ball.
3. Lock the ankle at contact so that the foot and leg form a right angle.
4. Use the entire body to produce force and transfer it forward into the ball.
5. Follow through in the direction of the intended flight letting the kicking leg carry the kicker off the ground.

Task Learning Experiences:
1. Place a ball on the tee and practice kicking concentrating on the mechanics of kicking. Use as many steps as needed. Repeat several times.
2. To achieve a high flight, the ball must be kicked under its center of gravity. Try kicking several times.
3. Kick five balls for height.
4. Kick five balls for distance. Does height affect distance?
5. Kick five balls to the right side, left, and center of the field. What adjustments are necessary for changing the direction of the ball flight?
6. Kick the ball five times for a distance of 20, 30, 40, or 50 yards.
7. In partners, A holds the ball and B concentrates on good kicking form. After a few successful and controlled kicks, add two or three preliminary steps prior to kicking. Repeat five times and reverse.

8. Kick three out of five balls over the goal bar from a distance of five, 10, 15, or 20 yards.
9. Repeat Task #8 from different angles.
10. In groups of four, A centers the ball to B who holds for C. C kicks while D retrieves. Repeat five times and rotate.
11. Repeat Task #10 from the extra point yardage line.

PUNT

Purpose:
To propel the ball strategically away from the defender's goal.

Skill Analysis:
1. Receive the center snap about waist high.
2. Rotate the ball so the laces are up.
3. Take a short step right, full step left, and kick right.
4. Drop the ball with both hands downward to kicking foot.
5. Keep arms out for balance after the drop.
6. Focus the eyes on the ball.
7. Contact the ball on the instep or lace part of the shoe.
8. Follow through in direction of intended flight.

Task Learning Experiences:
1. Punt several balls from a stationary position concentrating on the skill analysis.
2. Repeat Task #1 preceding the punt with a two-step approach (right, left, kick). Concentrate on force and transferring body momentum into ball. Repeat several times.
3. Punt five balls for distance. Try to achieve 20, 30, or 40 yards. Markers can be placed to designate yardage.
4. Stand in the center of the field and punt for accuracy. Try to place five punts toward the right sideline, the left sideline, and down the center.
5. Arrange targets on the field at various distances and angles. Punt and try to achieve 50 percent accuracy in punting close to the target area.
6. In partners or small groups, repeat Task #5. Compete trying to come the closest to the target. An element of scoring can be added.
7. In threes, A centers the ball to B who punts while C retrieves. Repeat five times and rotate.
8. Repeat Task #7 with C catching and running a few strides.
9. In groups of four, repeat Task #7 with the fourth player assuming a defensive position who rushes the punter after the hike.

NINE

Gymnastics

BALANCE BEAM

Purpose:
To maintain balance on a board (beam) with smoothness and fluency while executing mounts, locomotor movements, turns, static positions, and dismounts.

Skill Analysis:
1. Focus eyes at the end of the beam and not at the feet.
2. Learn the skills on the floor (on a line) before executing them on the beam.
3. Organize routines so they consist of a mount, locomotor skills, turns, and a dismount.
4. Walk beside the performer with a hand extended when spotting.
5. Use a low or medium beam for elementary level.
6. Surround the beam with mats for safety.

Task Learning Experiences:
1. Walk forward across the beam. Repeat three times.
2. Walk backward across the beam. Repeat three times.
3. Walk sideward across the beam. Repeat three times.
4. Walk forward dipping the foot below the side of the beam and then up. Repeat twice.
5. Step-hop across the beam. Repeat twice.
6. Skip across the beam. Repeat twice.
7. Gallop across the beam. Repeat twice.

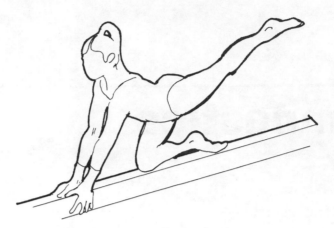

Knee scale

8. Balance bean bag on head while walking across the beam. Repeat twice.
9. Walk halfway across the beam and pivot turn on the toes (180°—½ turn). Repeat twice.
10. Balance on one foot on the beam and swing the other leg forward and backward. Swing the foot five times. Repeat three times.
11. Balance on the beam and hop on one foot. Repeat twice.
12. Repeat any of Tasks #1-#11 at a low level.
13. Repeat any of Tasks #1-#11 at a high level.
14. Balance on hands and knees on the beam raising a leg upward and backward (knee scale). Hold balance three seconds. Repeat three times.
15. Balance on the beam in a stork stand. (Balance on one leg with the other leg bent so the foot rests on the knee). Hold balance three seconds. Repeat twice.
16. Balance on the beam in an Arabesque. (Balance on right leg, straighten left leg and raise it backward and upward. Extend the right arm forward and the left arm backward.) Hold balance three seconds. Repeat three times.
17. Balance in a piked position (V-sit) while sitting on the beam. (Sitting, hands hold the top edge of the beam behind the hips. Bent knees are raised to the chest and then straightened and held.) Hold three seconds. Repeat twice.
18. While balancing on the beam, squat down (bend knees) and then return to a stand. Repeat five times.
19. Balance on the beam in a squat position and turn to face the opposite direction while squatting. Repeat five times.

Mounts
20. Front Lean Mount—Lean on the side of the beam and support the body. Swing one leg over to a straddle position. Hold three seconds. Repeat four times.

21. Squat Mount—Stand facing the side of the beam placing the hands on the beam. Jump up and forward placing the feet on the beam (between the hands) keeping the body in a squat position. Hold three seconds. Repeat four times.

Dismounts
22. Jump Dismount—Jump off the end of the beam landing in a controlled manner. Repeat four times.
23. Jump Half Turn Dismount—Jump off the end of the beam turning the body 180° before landing. Repeat four times.
24. Arch Jump Dismount—Jump, extend the body, swing the arms upward, and arch the back before landing. Repeat four times.
25. Straddle Jump Dismount — Jump off the side of the beam with the legs apart in a straddle position landing in a controlled, balanced position. Repeat four times.
26. Front Dismount—Squat down and extend the legs backward so the body forms a straight line. Kick the legs up and sideward

pushing off with the hands and landing on both feet beside the beam. Repeat four times.

27. Combine a mount, dismount, and several locomotor movements, turns, and static positions from Tasks #1-#26 into a routine.
28. Create a routine from Tasks #1-#26 and execute it to music.
29. Create a competitive routine 80 to 105 seconds in length using locomotor movements, turns, and static positions (hold three seconds each) as well as a mount and dismount from Tasks #1-#26.

SIDE HORSE VAULTING

Purpose:
To move the body over a horse or box using the hands for support (vault) and thus demonstrate the following components: approach (run), hurdle (take-off), horse contact (touch-off), and landing (dismount).

Skill Analysis:
1. Use a padded jumping box or a Swedish vaulting box in the lower grades.
2. Use mats or a landing pad on the far side of the box.
3. Station two spotters near the sides of the vaulting box.
4. Push the reuther board farther from the box to achieve greater speed and momentum.
5. Use a two foot spring (jump) on the board. The spring should be on the balls of the feet.
6. Learn to take-off first from just one step then add more steps. Increase to a slow run and finally progress to a maximum run.

Maximum speed should be reached approximately ten feet from the reuther board.

7. Bend the knees to absorb the force when landing from a vault. The landing must always be controlled and on both feet.
8. Bring the arms up into a "V-position" above the head after landing.
9. Touch the horse with the hands only momentarily on the contact.

Task Learning Experiences:

1. Take a short run toward the horse and practice the hurdle or jump on the reuther board. Just the hands contact the horse while the feet return to the board without executing any type of vault. Repeat 10 times.
2. Repeat Task #1 striving for height with the hips.
3. Knee to Stand Vault—Take a run, jump onto the board with both feet (hurdle), land on the horse on both knees (inside the hands), stand up, and jump off. Repeat five times.
4. Knee-Upspring Vault — Repeat the approach, take-off, and horse contact from Task #3. Instead of standing up for the dismount, use an upspring. Repeat five times. Upspring: Swing arms back and forth with force and jump from the knees to a stand on the floor by moving the legs forward.
5. Squat-On Vault—Take a run, jump onto the board, land on the horse with both feet together inside the hands (squat position), stand up, and jump off. Repeat eight times.
6. Repeat Task #5 jumping off the horse with the legs in a straddle position.
7. Repeat Task #5 turning in the air while jumping off the horse. Try a ¼, ½, or full turn in the air.
8. Repeat Task #5 executing another variation of the jump off the horse.
9. Straddle-On Vault—Take a run, jump onto the board, land on the horse with the legs spread apart outside the hands (straddle position). Push off with the hands and land with the feet together on the floor. Repeat four times.
10. Wolf-On Vault — Take a run, jump onto the board, bring one leg up to the horse in a squat position with the other leg extended straight out to the side. Pause and then jump to a controlled landing. Repeat three times.
11. Flank Vault—Take a run, jump onto the board, legs extended to one side and swing over the horse (weight on one hand only). The side of the body is parallel to the horse. The feet drop to the floor on the other side of the horse for the landing. Repeat three times.
12. Squat Vault—Take a run, jump onto the board, hands are placed on the horse while the legs are bent (squat) so they can pass between the arms without contacting the horse. The arms push

away from the horse and the body is extended before landing. Repeat three times.

13. Straddle Vault — Take a run, jump onto the board getting a lot of height with the hips. Hands are placed on the horse while the legs remain straight and in a straddle position as they pass over the horse without making contact. (Feet are outside of the hands.) The arms push away from the horse as the legs are brought together for the landing. Repeat three times.

14. Wolf Vault — Take a run, jump onto the board, hands contact the horse while the legs and body pass over the horse in the wolf position (one leg squatting and the other leg extended straight out to the side). The hands push away from the horse and the legs are brought together for the landing. Repeat three times.

15. Repeat Task #10 to the other side (reverse legs).

16. Repeat Task #14 to the other side (reverse legs).

17. Repeat Task #11 to the opposite side (leg swing).

18. Repeat any of Tasks #3-#17 concentrating on a balanced landing with the feet remaining together and with any extra steps being avoided. The arms shold be placed in a "V-position" above the head. This stance should be held (pause) before leaving the mat where the landing occurred.

19. Work on perfecting three vaults from Tasks #3-#17. Choose at least one of increased difficulty (Tasks #11-#17).

UNEVEN BARS

Purpose:
To demonstrate strength and flexibility on a two bar apparatus where one bar is fixated high and the other is low. Movements on the uneven bars include executing a mount, stunts on one bar, stunts going to the high bar, and a dismount.

Skill Analysis:
1. Lower the high bar to a point where the student's feet are within a foot of the floor when hanging (for the lower grades).
2. Surround the bars with mats.
3. Use two spotters. They should constantly be aware of preventing any part of the student's body from landing on the floor before the feet.
4. Use three types of grips for uneven bar skills:
   4.1 Overgrip—thumbs on the inside of the grip
   4.2 Undergrip—thumbs on the outside of the grip
   4.3 Mixed grip — one hand in an overgrip and the other in an undergrip
   The thumb should point in the direction the body is going to move except for the grip in the front hip circle and the forward roll.

5. Extend the knees and point the toes for most stunts on the uneven bars.

Task Learning Experiences:
Mounts
1. Front Support—Jump up and grasp (overgrip) the low bar and rest (balance) the thighs on the bar while keeping the head and shoulders forward. Hold for six seconds. Repeat three times.
2. Pull Over to Front Support—Grasp the low bar (overgrip) and swing the legs upward and around the bar to a front support. The upper torso should drop back as the arms flex (bend) to pull the body around. Hold for six seconds. Repeat three times.
3. Swing to Tuck—Jump to a hang on the high bar using an overgrip. Swing the legs back and forth and then forward with force (tucked position) so both legs can pass over the low bar and the upper legs can rest on the low bar. Hold for six seconds. Repeat three times.

Stunts on One Bar
4. Swan Balance — Execute a front support and release the grip (bring the arms overhead) and balance on the thighs. Hold for three seconds. Repeat three times.
5. Side Stride Support — Execute a front support and bring one leg up and over the low bar by extending it to the side (stride position). Place the weight on the hands and raise the body so it is off the bar. Hold for three seconds. Repeat three times.
6. Push Away — Execute a front support and throw the legs back

ward away from the bar. The legs then return to the front support position on the bar. Push away three times. Repeat twice.

7. Shoot Through — Execute a push-away and as the legs are thrown backward bring one leg upward and forward over the bar ending in a stride position. Hold for three seconds. Repeat three times.

8. Back Hip Circle—Execute a front support. Push away from the bar and as the hips touch the bar, throw the legs forward and upward rotating around the bar. Adjust the grip of the hands and return to a front support. Repeat four times.

9. Side Stride Circle — Execute a side stride support (Task #5) and shift the body weight forward by leaning with the forward leg thus rotating under and around the bar. Momentum can be gained by lifting the back leg and arching the back. Return to the starting positions. Repeat four times.

10. Front Hip Circle — Execute a front support and shift the body weight forward by leaning forward with the chest. Flex the body at the waist and bend the elbows when inverted for a full body rotation of the bar. Return to the starting position. Repeat four times.

Stunts Going to the High Bar

11. Rise to Front Support — Overgrip the high bar with the feet resting on the low bar. Straighten the legs and push down on the high bar with the arms ending in a front support. Hold three seconds. Repeat three times.

12. Pull over to High Bar — Overgrip the high bar (body facing the low bar) with one leg extended and the other leg bent and resting on the low bar. Swing the extended leg backward and upward over the high bar keeping the arms bent. Push off with the flexed leg and rotate to a front support. Hold three seconds. Repeat three times.

Dismounts

13. Quarter Turn—From a stride position on the low bar, lift the back leg sideways and up over the bar executing a ¼ turn and landing on the mat. The weight is supported on one arm which maintains contact with the bar as the other arm is released. Repeat five times.

14. Swing Under — From a front support on the low bar, lower the body behind the bar while raising the legs upward. Once the torso is under the bar, extend the legs upward, forward, and then outward followed by a release of the bar with the hands. Land with the arms extended overhead. Repeat five times.

15. Forward roll — From a front support on the high or low bar, bend forward at the waist, roll over the bar, and extend the legs down toward the ground. The arms can be released for the dismount. Repeat five times.

16. Execute the following uneven bar routine:
    16.1 Mount to a front support (hold three seconds).
    16.2 Push away from the bar three times.
    16.3 Swan balance (three seconds).
    16.4 Front hip circle.
    16.5 Pull over to high bar (hold front support three seconds).
    16.6 Forward roll dismount.

17. Choose stunts from Task #1-#15 and combine them into a routine. The stunts should be chosen so that smoothness and continuity are achieved when moving from one stunt to another.

PARALLEL BARS

Purpose:

To demonstrate controlled strength and flexibility while executing a mount, various stunts, and a dismount on two bars fixated in a parallel position.

Skill Analysis:

1. Use two spotters—one on each side of the bars. Spot from under the bars.

2. Use medium height bars for the lower grades (elementary size bars are below shoulder height).
3. Keep the head facing straight ahead while executing a stunt.
4. Keep the body straight with the back arched for most stunts.
5. Surround the bars with mats for safety.
6. Demonstrate that the arms can support the body before attempting any traveling stunts.

Task Learning Experiences:

1. Straight Arm Support — Jump up to the bars so straight arms support the body (elbows locked). Hold eight seconds. Repeat three times.
2. Hand Walk — While in a straight arm support, take "steps" forward with the hands (shift body weight from one hand to the other). Hand walk the length of the bars. Repeat twice.
3. Repeat Task #2 "walking" backward.
4. Front Hook—While in a straight arm support, swing legs forward and up resting the feet on the bars. Straighten the body then release the legs for the dismount. Repeat five times.
5. Rear Hook — Repeat Task #4 swinging the legs backward and up.
6. Straight Arm Support Swing— While in a straight arm support, swing the body back and forth, then dismount. Swing six times. Repeat twice.
7. Straddle Seat — While in a straight arm support, swing the legs forward and over the bars into a straddle position. Balance on the upper thighs. Balance for three seconds. Push the body up with the arms and swing the legs down, then dismount. Repeat three times.
8. Straddle Travel — Repeat Task #7 eliminating the dismount. Swing the legs down and up to a new straddle position. Travel the length of the bars, then dismount. Repeat twice.
9. Inverted Hang — While holding the bars, pull into a tucked upside down position. Extend the legs and hang. Hang for three seconds. Dismount by tucking the body and returning to a stand. Repeat twice.
10. Skin the Cat—Hold the bars, tuck up the legs and hips and bring them over the head passing through the bars. After lowering the legs, release the hands and drop to a stand. Repeat three times.
11. Front Leaning Support — Stand by the side of the bars. Jump onto the bars and rest the body on the abdominal area. Keep the arms straight and the body arched. Hold the support three seconds. Repeat four times.
12. Riding Seat — From a straight arm support, bring the legs up and swing them over one bar. One leg (leg of side closest to the bar) is bent and the opposite leg points straight backward. The hands stay on the bars to aid in balance. Hold three seconds. Repeat twice.

13. Side Stride — Execute a straddle seat then quarter turn the body to either side. The body is across the bar with the front knee bent around the bar and the back leg resting on the thigh muscle. Hold three seconds. Repeat twice.
14. Forward Roll — From a straddle seat, reach forward and grasp the bars bending the elbows out to the side. Roll forward by raising the hips, rounding the back, and rolling onto the upper arms. The legs remain straddled so that the thighs land on the bars and roll back into a straddle seat. Repeat four times.

Mounts
15. Straight Arm Support Mount—Jump or have a spotter lift the student to the straight arm support position. Hold three seconds. Repeat four times.
16. Straddle Seat Mount — Jump and raise the body to a straddle seat from a straight arm support mount. Hold three seconds. Repeat four times.

Dismounts
17. Rear Vault Dismount — From a straight arm support, swing both legs forward over the right bar. Simultaneously hold the right bar with the left hand and release the right hand. Land inside the bars. Repeat four times.
18. Front Vault Dismount — Repeat Task #17 swinging both legs backward over the bar. Land beside the bars with the hand nearest the bar regripping it. Repeat four times.
19. Combine a mount, several stunts, and a dismount from Tasks #1-#18 into a routine.
20. Perform the following routine:
    20.1 Straight arm support mount (hold three seconds).
    20.2 Hand walk forward halfway across the bars.
    20.3 Hand walk backward halfway across the bars.
    20.4 Straddle seat (hold three seconds).
    20.5 Side stride (hold three seconds).
    20.6 Straddle travel to end of the bars.
    20.7 Straight arm support (hold three seconds).
    20.8 Front vault dismount.

LOW HORIZONTAL BAR

Purpose:
To execute various hangs and swings on a low bar and thus demonstrate arm and shoulder strength.

Skill Analysis:
1. Use the standard grip in which the thumb goes around the bar (opposed-thumb grip). The back of the hands face the performer (overgrip).

2. Dismount by landing with the knees bent and on the balls of the feet.
3. Place mats or a landing pad under the bar.
4. Use two spotters (especially when executing inverted hangs).
5. Do not exceed five feet in height and have a circumference of greater than four inches for the horizontal bar when used in the lower grades.

Task Learning Experiences:
1. Extended Arm Hang — Grasp the bar (overgrip) and hang with straight arms. Hold for six seconds. Repeat twice.
2. Flexed Arm Hang — Grasp the bar (overgrip) and hang with the arms in a bent elbow position. Hold for six seconds. Repeat three times.
3. Front Swing—Execute a flexed arm hang and swing the legs forward from the hips keeping the body straight. Swing four times. Repeat three times.
4. Repeat Task #3 dismounting at the front of the swing (after four swings).
5. Repeat Task #3 dismounting at the back of the swing (after four swings).
6. Side Swing — Execute a flexed arm hang and swing the legs sideward from the hips. Swing six times. Repeat twice.
7. Sloth Hang — Facing the end of the bar, grasp the bar with both hands and hook the knees over the bar. Dismount by continuing to grasp the bar and then unhooking the knees. Hold the hang for 10 seconds. Repeat twice.
8. Tuck Position Hang—Execute a flexed arm hang and raise bent knees toward the chest. Hold for three seconds. Repeat three times.
9. Pike Position Hang — Execute a flexed arm hang and bring straight legs up so they extend at right angles to the body with the toes pointed. Hold for three seconds. Repeat three times.
10. "V" Position Hang — Repeat Task #9 bringing straight legs up to the face. Hold for three seconds. Repeat three times.
11. Front Hand Support—Grasp the bar (overgrip) and pull the body up so the hips rest and balance on the bar. Hold the balance for 10 seconds. Repeat four times.
12. Knee Hang — Grasp the bar (overgrip) and bring both legs up through the bar. Release the hands and hang from the back of the bent knees. Dismount by regrasping the bar and dropping the knees. Hold the hang for eight seconds. Repeat twice.
13. Knee Hang Swing — Repeat Task #12 swinging forward and backward on the knees.
14. One Knee Hang — Repeat Task #12 with the hooking of only one knee over the bar.
15. One Knee Mount — Execute a one knee hang. Extend the free leg backward bringing the hips toward the bar while extending

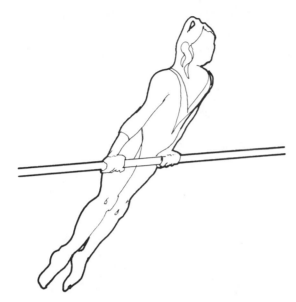

Front hand support

the arms. Pull up to a side stride position on the bar with one knee on the bar and the other knee extended. Hold eight seconds. Repeat three times.

16. One Knee Circle — Execute a one knee mount and swing the extended leg back and forth while the other leg is hooked at the knee. The straight (extended) leg is then swung forward with force as the upper body drops backward. The body completely circles the bar and returns to the one knee mount. Repeat four times.

17. Pull-Over — Grasp the bar (overgrip) and swing the legs upward and around the bar to a front hand support position (Task #11). The upper body should drop back as the arms flex to pull the body around. Repeat four times.

18. Pullup — Grasp the bar (overgrip or undergrip) and raise the body so the chin touches the bar. Then lower the body. Do five pullups in a row. Repeat twice.

19. Skin the Cat — Grasp the bar (overgrip) and pull the feet up between the arms under the bar. The legs are then lowered and extended toward the ground. This can be used as a dismount by releasing the bar at this point or the legs can be brought back up and over thus reversing the sequence. Repeat three times.

20. Bird's Nest — Grasp the bar (overgrip) and bring both legs up through the arms and hook the knees on the bar. Arch back and slide the legs so the heels rest on the bar. The arms are held straight. Repeat twice.

21. Forward Roll — Execute a front hand support (Task #11) and bend forward at the waist rolling over the bar and causing the

legs to extend down toward the ground. Dismount by releasing the bar. Repeat four times.

22. Execute the following low horizontal bar routine:
    22.1 Mount to a flexed arm hang (three seconds).
    22.2 Front swing back and forth three times.
    22.3 One knee hang (three seconds).
    22.4 One knee mount (hold side stride three seconds).
    22.5 Front hand support (three seconds).
    22.6 Forward roll dismount.
23. Choose stunts from Tasks #1-#21 and combine into a routine. The stunts should be chosen so that smoothness and continuity are achieved when moving from one stunt to another.

STILL RINGS

Purpose:
To keep two parallel, suspended rings as motionless as possible while executing various hangs and stunts. Strength and flexibility are the two components demonstrated in still ring performances.

Skill Analysis:
1. Use two spotters. Each can hold the student's hands on the rings while in the early learning stages.
2. Place the rings as low as possible with mats or a landing pad under them.
3. Begin with the rings as motionless as possible in order to maintain their stillness throughout the routine.
4. Land with the knees bent and in a controlled stance following the dismount.
5. Demonstrate adequate arm and abdominal strength prior to executing the various stunts.

Task Learning Experiences:
1. Extended Arm Hand — Grasp the rings and hang with straight arms. Hold for six seconds. Repeat twice.
2. Flexed Arm Hang — Grasp the rings and hang with the arms in a bent elbow position. Hold for six seconds. Repeat three times.
3. Tuck Position (knee lift) — Execute a flexed arm hang and raise bent knees toward the chest. Hold for three seconds. Repeat twice.
4. Pike Position — Execute a flexed arm hang and bring straight legs up so they extend at right angles to the body (horizontal) with the toes pointed. Hold for three seconds. Repeat twice.
5. "V" Position—Repeat Task #4 bringing straight legs up to face.
6. Bicycle — Execute a flexed arm hang and move knees as if riding a bicycle. Repeat three times, each time bicycling for six seconds.

7. Pullups — Raise and lower the body while grasping the rings thus alternating between a flexed and extended arm hang. The chin should touch the hands each time. Do five pullups. Repeat twice.

8. Inverted Hang — Execute a tuck position then raise the body upward by straightening the legs over the hands. Dismount by returning to the tuck position and then lowering the legs. Note: The legs may be wrapped around each ring suspension as the upside down position is held. Hold the inverted hang three seconds. Repeat twice.

9. Repeat Task #8 without wrapping the feet around the ring suspensions. Always look straight down at the ground while executing an inverted hang.

10. Bird's Nest — Execute an inverted hang and hook the toes in the rings so the chest is arched and the head is held high. Hold for three seconds, then return to the inverted position for a dismount. Repeat twice.

11. Pike Inverted Hang — Execute an inverted hang and bend the torso at the hips so the body is upside down and the legs extend at right angles to the body. Focus the eyes on the knees. Hold for three seconds. Repeat twice.

12. Skin the Cat — Execute a flexed arm hang, kick the legs overhead and roll until the legs are extending down. This can be used as a dismount by releasing the rings at this point or the legs can be brought back up and over thus reversing the sequence. Repeat three times.

13. Execute the following still rings routine:
    13.1   Mount to a flexed arm hang (hold three seconds).
    13.2   Do three pull-ups.
    13.3   Tuck position (three seconds).
    13.4   Inverted hang (three seconds).
    13.5   Bird's nest (three seconds).
    13.6   Flexed arm hang (three seconds).
    13.7   Skin the cat dismount.

14. Combine several stunts from Tasks #1-#12 into a routine. The stunts must flow smoothly and continuously from one to the other. The rings should be held quite motionless.

TEN

Rhythmic Gymnastics

BALLS

Purpose:
To manipulate a ball using rolling, swinging, bouncing, and throwing patterns of movement in a smooth, flowing manner to music with a ¾ time signature.

Skill Analysis:
1. Rest the ball on the hand and avoid grasping it for most rhythmic ball activities.
2. Toss the ball using motion from the shoulders rather than the arms when executing rhythmic ball activities.
3. Catch the ball with the fingertips and let it settle into the palm when receiving the ball.
4. Swing and roll the ball by holding the ball with a wrist grasp (ball lies between the palm and forearm).
5. Use a ball which is approximately six inches in diameter for the rhythmic ball activities.
6. Use music with a ¾ time signature for rhythmic ball activities.

Task Learning Experiences:
1. From a stand, roll the ball in front of the body along the floor releasing the ball from a right-handed wrist grasp (hold the ball in between the palm and forearm) and receiving the ball with a left-handed wrist grasp. Reverse and repeat five times in each direction.

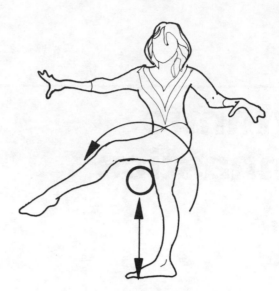

Ball Movements—See Task #13

2. From a sitting position (legs extended), roll the ball under the legs (V-seat) along the floor releasing the ball from a right-handed wrist grasp and receiving the ball with a left-handed wrist grasp. Reverse and repeat five times in each direction.
3. From a sitting position (legs extended), roll the ball around the legs with the right hand, change the ball to the left hand and roll the ball around the back of the body. Begin and end with a right-handed wrist grasp. Repeat five times.
4. From a sitting position (legs extended) with the legs lifted off the ground, place the ball on the feet and roll the ball down the legs receiving the ball with a two-handed wrist grasp. Repeat 10 times.
5. From a standing position with the right arm extended to the side and the ball grasped in the right wrist, allow the ball to roll along the arm to the shoulder. Let the ball drop to the floor behind the body and turn to catch the ball with the left hand after the bounce. Reverse using the other arm. Repeat five rolls on each arm.
6. From a standing position with both arms extended in front and the ball grasped in both wrists, allow the ball to roll down the arms toward the chest. Let the ball drop to the floor in front of the body, catching the ball with both hands after the bounce. Repeat 10 times.
7. From a standing position with the ball in a right-handed wrist grasp, swing the right arm upward, change the ball to the left hand, then swing the left arm downward. Repeat five times in each direction, transferring the ball back and forth.
8. Repeat Task #7 swinging the arm (ball) in a circle prior to changing to the opposite hand.

9. From a standing position with the ball in a right-handed wrist grasp, swing the right arm across the body to the left side and change the ball to the left hand. Swing the ball back over to the right side and return the ball to the right hand. Repeat five times transferring the ball back and forth.

10. From a standing position with the ball in a right-handed wrist grasp, swing the right arm across the body to the left side and change the ball to the left hand. Swing the ball around behind the body and change back to the right hand. Repeat five times.

11. From a standing position, hold the ball with both hands in front, bounce the ball hard, turn completely around (360°) and retrieve the ball with a two-handed catch after the bounce. Repeat five times.

12. From a standing position with the ball in the right hand, bounce the ball in front of the body and catch it with the left hand. Reverse and repeat five times in each direction.

13. Repeat Task #12 raising the right leg so the ball bounces under the leg.

14. From a standing position with the ball in both hands in front, bounce the ball and swing the arms up and out to the sides. Return the arms to the center again to catch the ball. Bend the knees with each bounce. Repeat 10 times.

15. From a standing position with the ball in the right hand, throw the ball upward (over the head) and catch the ball with both hands. Return the ball to the right hand again. Repeat five times then reverse using the left hand.

16. Repeat Task #15 catching the ball with the left hand instead of both hands.

17. From a standing position with the ball in both hands in front of the body, bring the ball down low and throw it high using the entire body for momentum. Catch the ball with the fingers and return to the starting position. Repeat five times.

18. Repeat Task #17 crossing the arms prior to catching the ball then uncrossing them as the ball approaches the body so the ball is ready to be thrown again.

19. From a standing position with the ball in a right-handed wrist grasp and both arms extended to the sides, throw the ball up so it goes over the left shoulder and is caught with the left hand. Repeat five times then reverse using a left-handed wrist grasp.

20. Using music that has a lively ¾ rhythm such as a waltz, combine four tasks from Tasks #1-#19 into a short sequence. One task should be chosen from Tasks #1-#6, another task should be chosen from Tasks #11-#14, and one task should be chosen from Tasks #15-#19.

21. Repeat Task #20 using four different tasks, one from each of the mentioned groups.

22. Combine a variety of ball movements to music to create a rhythmic routine. Concentrate on flowing smoothly from one ball movement to another and keeping in rhythm to the music.

23. Demonstrate the ball routine from Task #22 to the class.
24. Perform a ball routine within a 40′ × 40′ area, moving the body throughout the entire area during the routine. (These are some of the guidelines which qualify the routine for competition.)

CLUBS

Purpose:
To manipulate a club or clubs using swinging and circling patterns of movement in a smooth, flowing manner to music with a ¾ time signature.

Skill Analysis:
1. Learn to execute the club movements with the nondominant hand as well as the dominant hand.
2. Flex the knees when the club head is down.
3. Extend the knees when the club head is up.
4. Keep the palms of the hand down for a regular grip.
5. Keep the palms of the hand up, resting the club on an extended index finger for a reverse grip.
6. Use music with a ¾ time signature for rhythmic club activities.

Task Learning Experiences:
One Club Movements
1. With the arms at the sides, swing the club in the right hand (regular grip — palms down) and exchange hands bringing the club down in the left hand. Reverse and repeat five times in each direction.
2. With the arms extended out to the sides, swing the club across the body in the right hand (regular grip) and receive the club in the left hand. Repeat swinging left across to right. Practice five times in each direction.
3. With the arms at the sides, swing the club down, back and over the head in the right hand (regular grip) and exchange hands when the club is extended forward in front. With the club in the left hand, swing the club down and back over the head to the front forward position again. Exchange hands returning the club to the right hand. Repeat five times.
4. Repeat Task #3 swinging in the opposite direction—up, over the head and back.
5. Extending the right arm above the head with the club in a right-handed regular grip, flex the elbow and cause the club to drop down and around in a circle in front of the head. Repeat using the left hand. Practice five times with each hand.
6. Extending the right arm above the head with the club in a right-handed reverse grip (palms up), flex the elbow and cause the

club to drop down and around in a circle in back of the head. Repeat using the left hand. Practice five times with each hand.

7. Combine Tasks #5 and #6 to make a circle in front of the head followed by one in back of the head. This will appear as a figure eight pattern.

8. Extending the right arm to the side with a club in a right-handed regular grip, flex the elbow and make a forward circle at the side. Repeat using the left hand. Practice five times with each hand.

9. Extending the right arm to the side with the club in a right-handed reverse grip, flex the elbow and make a backward circle at the side. Repeat using the left hand. Practice five times with each hand.

10. Combine Tasks #8 and #9 making a forward circle then reversing the grip and making a backward circle.

11. Extending the right arm out in front with the club in a right-handed regular grip, make a circle in front of the body. Repeat using the left hand. Practice five times with each hand.

12. Extending the right arm behind with the club in a right-handed regular grip, flex the elbow and make a circle in back of the body. Repeat using the left hand. Practice five times with each hand.

13. Combine Tasks #11 and #12 circling down in front of the body and up in back of the body. Repeat using the left hand. Practice five times with each hand.

Two Club Movements

14. Extend the right arm above the head using a regular club grip and extend the left arm down at the side using regular club grip. Swing the right arm forward and the left arm backward in side circles simultaneously. Repeat 10 times.

15. Extending both arms straight out to the right side using a regular club grip, make a circle in front of the body with both clubs simultaneously. Repeat five times.

16. Extending both arms straight out to the sides (one to the right and one to the left) using a regular club grip, both clubs forward, then change to a reverse grip and circle both clubs backward. Repeat five times in each direction.

17. Extending both arms straight out to the sides (one to the right and one to the left) using a regular grip with the right hand and a reverse grip with the left hand, make a front of the head circle with the right hand (see Task #5) and a back of the head circle with the left hand (see Task #6) simultaneously. Repeat five times.

18. Using music with a ¾ rhythm such as a waltz, combine four tasks from Tasks #1-#13 into a short sequence. One task should be chosen from Tasks #1-#4 and three tasks from Tasks #5-#13.

19. Repeat Task #18 using four different tasks from Tasks #1-#13.

20. Repeat Task #18 using the four tasks described in Tasks #14-#17.
21. Repeat Task #18 creating at least two club movements not presented in Tasks #1-#17.
22. Combine a variety of club movements to music to create a rhythmic routine. Concentrate on flowing smoothly from one club movement to another and keeping in rhythm to the music.
23. Demonstrate the club routine from Task #22 to the class.
24. Perform a club routine to music within a 40' × 40' area, moving the body throughout the entire area during the routine. (These are some of the guidelines which qualify the routine for competition.)

HOOPS

Purpose:
To manipulate a hoop using swinging, rolling, spinning, circling, throwing, and jumping patterns of movement in a smooth, flowing manner to music with a ¾ time signature.

Skill Analysis:
1. Use the entire body to enhance a hoop routine. For example, the arm that is not holding the hoop should be positioned to complement the hoop movement.
2. Use either an inside (under grip) or outside (over grip) grip for hoop activities.

Hoop Movements—See Task #1

3. Use a large space for practicing hoop routines in order to allow for full body movement.
4. Use hoops with a smaller diameter than the standard 27 inches for the lower grades.
5. Use music with a ¾ time signature that has various interesting modulations for the rhythmic hoop activities.

Task Learning Experiences:

1. Holding the hoop to the side in one hand with an inside grip, swing the hoop forward (up) and back (down). Repeat using the opposite hand. Practice five times with each hand.
2. Holding the hoop down at the side in one hand with an inside grip, swing the hoop forward (up), change hands and swing the hoop back down to the other side. Reverse and repeat five times in each direction.
3. Holding the hoop straight out in front of the body (parallel to the ground) with both hands in an inside grip, swing the hoop from the right side to the left. Turn the hoop over (outside grip) and swing the hoop around behind the body. Turn the hoop over again returning it to the starting position. Repeat five times.
4. While stabilizing the hoop vertically on the ground with one hand, use the opposite hand to push the hoop so that it rolls. Run a few steps and receive the hoop with one hand again. Practice for five minutes.
5. Holding the hoop with one hand to the side using an inside grip, swing the hoop forward low and release it while it is on the floor at the end of the swing. Use the wrist to pull the hand toward the body quickly during the release. This will cause the hoop to swing out then return as a roll. (This puts a back spin on the hoop.) Practice for 10 minutes.
6. Holding the hoop vertically on the ground with one hand, use the fingers to turn the hoop into a spin by itself. Remove the hand and let it spin. Repeat five times.

NOTE: For Tasks #7-#12 the grasp is released and wrist action is used to circle the hoop on the fingers or back of the hand.

7. Holding the hoop in one hand, extend the arm straight out to the side and make a circle with the hoop to the side. Repeat using the opposite hand. Practice for one minute with each hand.
8. Holding the hoop in the right hand in front of the body, make a circle with the hoop then change to the left hand and bring the hoop to the side. Reverse and repeat five times in each direction.
9. Holding the hoop in the right hand, circle the hoop in back of the body receiving the hoop in the left hand. Reverse and repeat five times in each direction.
10. Holding the hoop in the right hand in front of the body, make a circle with the hoop then receive it in the left hand. Continue the

movement by circling the hoop in back of the body with the left hand and receive it in the right hand again. (Hoop circles 360° around the body). Repeat five times.

11. Holding the hoop in the right hand, extend the right arm straight out to the side and circle the hoop on the right side. Bring the right arm across in front of the body and circle the hoop on the left side. Return the right arm back to the right side completing a figure eight pattern. Repeat five times.

12. Holding the hoop in the right hand, extend the arm above the head and circle the hoop around the hand. Repeat five times and change to the left hand.

13. Holding the hoop in one hand out in front of the body using an inside grip, throw the hoop up using wrist action and catch it in the opposite hand. Reverse and repeat five times in each direction.

14. Holding the hoop straight out to the side with one hand using an inside grip, throw the hoop over the head and catch it on the other side of the body with the opposite hand. Reverse and repeat five times in each direction.

15. Holding the hoop in front of the body so the hoop is parallel to the ground, swing the hoop down and jump through it, bringing the hoop behind and over the head again (as if jumping rope). Repeat for two minutes.

16. Repeat Task #15 swinging the hoop back over the head and behind the body as if jumping rope backward.

17. Spin the hoop as in Task #6 and jump over the hoop while it spins. Repeat five times.

18. Roll the hoop as in Task #4 and jump through the hoop while it rolls. Repeat five times.

19. Repeat Task #18 jumping over the hoop.

20. Put a back spin roll on the hoop as in Task #5 and jump over the hoop while it rolls back. Repeat five times.

21. Using music with a ¾ rhythm such as a waltz, combine five tasks from Tasks #1-#20 into a short sequence. One task should be chosen from Tasks #1-#3, another task should be chosen from Tasks #4-#5, another should be chosen from Tasks #7-#12, another should be chosen from Tasks #13-#14, and one should be chosen from Tasks #15-#20.

22. Repeat Task #21 using five other tasks, one from each of the mentioned groups.

23. Combine a variety of hoop movements to music to create a rhythmic routine. Concentrate on flowing smoothly from one hoop movement to another and keeping in rhythm to the music.

24. Demonstrate the hoop routine from Task #23 to the class.

25. Perform a hoop routine to music within a 40′ × 40′ area moving the body throughout the entire area during the routine. (These are some of the guidelines which qualify the routine for competition.)

RIBBONS

Purpose:
To manipulate a ribbon (on a stick) using arc, circular, figure eight, snake, and spiral patterns of movement in a smooth, flowing manner to music with a ¾ time signature.

Skill Analysis:
1. Explore ways of manipulating the ribbon prior to executing set patterns.
2. Maintain a rhythmic flow with the ribbon in order to avoid its collapse on the floor.
3. Avoid making any whiplike sounds with the ribbon so the visual aesthetic quality of the activity is emphasized.
4. Use ribbons that are shorter in length than the standard 20 feet for the lower grades.
5. Use music with a ¾ time signature when introducing rhythmic ribbon activities.

Task Learning Experiences:
1. Move the ribbon in various ways in order to become familiarized with its motion. Repeat for five minutes.
2. Swing the ribbon from one side of the body to the other in an arc pattern in front of the body. Repeat for one minute.
3. Repeat Task #2 behind the body.
4. Swing the ribbon in an arc pattern beside the body (left or right side) from front to back then reverse back to front. Repeat for one minute.
5. Swing the ribbon in a horizontal wave pattern at a high level. Repeat for one minute.
6. Repeat Task #5 at a medium level.
7. Repeat Task #5 at a low level.
8. Swing the ribbon in a circular pattern (full circle) in front of the body. Repeat for one minute.
9. Repeat Task #8 to the side of the body (left or right side).
10. Repeat Task #8 over the head.
11. Repeat Task #8 under the feet and jump over the ribbon.
12. Swing the ribbon in a figure eight pattern vertically in front of the body. Repeat for one minute.
13. Repeat Task #12 beside the body (left or right side).
14. Swing the ribbon in a figure eight pattern horizontally in front of the body. Repeat for one minute.
15. Repeat Task #14 beside the body (left or right side).
16. Swing the ribbon like a snake parallel to the floor in front of the body. Repeat for one minute.
17. Repeat Task #16 behind the body.
18. Repeat Task #16 above the head.

19. Swing the ribbon in a spiral pattern in front of the body by rotating the hand in continuous small circles. Repeat for one minute.
20. Repeat Task #19 perpendicular to the floor spiraling down.
21. Repeat Task #19 perpendicular to the floor spiraling up.
22. Using slow tempo music that has a ¾ time signature, combine four tasks from Tasks #2-#21 into a short sequence.
23. Repeat Task #22 using four different tasks.
24. Combine a variety of patterns to music to create a ribbon routine. Concentrate on flowing smoothly from one pattern to another and keeping in rhythm to the music.
25. Demonstrate the ribbon routine from Task #24 to the class.
26. Perform a ribbon routine to music within a 40′ × 40′ area moving the body throughout the entire area during the routine. Attempt to interchange the ribbon from the right to left hand at various times. (These are some of the guidelines which qualify the routine for competition.)

(NOTE: Ribbons can be constructed by attaching 20 feet by 2-inch wide ribbon to a ⅜ inch by 2-feet long dowel rod. The ribbon can be attached to the dowel rod by using strong thread which passes through a small hole made in the end of the rod.)

ROPES

Purpose:
To manipulate a rope using jumping, swinging, circling, and winding patterns of movement in a smooth, flowing manner to music with a ¾ time signature.

Skill Analysis:

1. Jump lightly on the toes to avoid making noise when jumping rope.
2. Fold the rope in half and hold the two ends together in one or both hand(s) when swinging and circling the rope.
3. Wrap the rope around a body part by using a quick rotating action which causes the rope to wind.
4. Use a rope length which is appropriate to the size of the participant. The rope should reach the arms as they are extended out to the sides when standing on the center of the rope with one foot.
5. Use music with a ¾ time signature for rhythmic rope activities.

Task Learning Experiences:

1. Jump forward over the rope as it is turning from back to front. Take off from both feet and land on both feet. Repeat 10 times.
2. Repeat Task #1 taking off from both feet and landing on one foot.
3. Repeat Task #1 taking off from one foot and landing on the same foot.
4. Repeat Task #1 taking off from one foot and landing on both feet.
5. Repeat Task #1 taking off from one foot and landing on the other
6. Repeat Task #1 crossing the arms during the jump (turn the rope with the hands far out at the sides).
7. Repeat Task #1 crossing the legs during the jump.
8. Repeat Task #1 rocking between the front and back feet during the jump.
9. Repeat Task #1 skipping in place.
10. Jump backward over the rope as it is turning from front to back. Take off from both feet and land on both feet. Repeat 10 times.
11. In partners facing each other, A turns the rope as both A and B jump together. Repeat 10 times.
12. Repeat Task #11 with both A and B facing the same direction.

NOTE: For Tasks #13-#22 the rope is folded in half and the two ends held in one or both hand(s) (swinging and circling).

13. Holding the rope in both hands, make a forward circle to one side (right or left). Repeat five times.
14. Repeat Task #13 with a backward circle to one side (right or left).
15. Holding the rope in both hands, make a forward circle to the right side, switch to the left side, then back to the right side again in a figure eight pattern. Repeat five times.
16. Holding the rope in both hands, make a circle over the head (as if lassoing). Repeat five times.
17. Holding the rope in one hand, circle the rope along the floor,

jumping over the rope circle as it approaches the feet. Repeat 10 times.

18. Holding the rope in one hand, make a circle in front of the body then change hands circling back again. Repeat five times in each direction.

19. Holding the rope in one hand with the arm extended straight out to the side, quickly rotate (turn) the entire arm forward allowing the rope to wind (wrap) around the arm. Reverse the direction of the rotation and unwind the rope. Repeat five times.

20. Repeat Task #19 extending the arm overhead.

21. Holding the rope in one hand, swing the rope around the waist gathering momentum for the winding (wrapping) by snapping the wrists as the hand is brought toward the waist. Repeat five times.

22. Repeat Task #21 winding the rope around a leg.

23. Using music with a ¾ rhythm such as a waltz, combine five tasks from Tasks #1-#22 into a short sequence. Ten tasks should be chosen from Tasks #1-#12, two tasks should be chosen from Tasks #13-#18, and one task should be chosen from Tasks #19-#22.

24. Repeat Task #23 using five different tasks, one from each of the mentioned groups.

25. Combine a variety of rope movements to music to create a rhythmic routine. Concentrate on flowing smoothly from one rope movement to another and keeping in rhythm to the music.

26. Demonstrate the rope routine from Task #25 to the class attempting to perform with precision.

27. Perform a rope routine to music within a 40' × 40' area moving the body throughout the entire area during the routine. (These are some of the guidelines which qualify the routine for competition.)

WANDS

Purpose:
To manipulate a wand using swinging, circling, jumping, throwing and other various patterns of movement in a smooth, flowing manner to music with a ¾ time signature.

Skill Analysis:
1. Hold the wand either at shoulder distance apart or at the ends depending on what the movement requires.

2. Use a large area with sufficient space for executing wand movements so another student is not injured.

3. Provide opportunity for students to create their own wand movements.

4. Use a wand which is shorter in length than the standard three feet for the lower grades.
5. Use music with a ¾ time signature for rhythmic wand activities.

Task Learning Experiences:

1. From a standing position, grasp the wand at the ends, jump forward over the wand, then jump backward over the wand to the original position. Repeat five times in both directions.
2. From a standing position, grasp the wand at the ends, let it drop, then catch it. Repeat five times.
3. From a standing position, grasp the wand at the ends, throw the wand up and catch it. Complete five successful catches.
4. Repeat Task #3 turning the body completely around (360°) before catching the wand.
5. Repeat Task #3 throwing the wand up with one hand and catching it with the other.
6. From a standing position with the arms extended straight out to the sides, grasp the wand at one end in the right hand and swing it across the body in front, catching it with the left hand. Swing the wand back to the right hand again. Repeat five times in each direction.
7. From a standing position with the arms extended straight out to the sides, grasp the wand at one end in the right hand, then _____ with the wand, receiving it with the left hand. Circle the wand with the left hand and receive it back into the right hand again. Repeat five times in each direction.
8. From a standing position with the arms extended straight out to the sides, grasp the wand at one end with the right hand then swing the wand behind the lower back and receive it with the left hand. Swing the wand back to the right hand in the same manner. Repeat five times in each direction.
9. From a standing position holding the wand with one hand and as it stands on end, swing the right leg over the wand, catching it before it falls. Repeat swinging the left leg over. Practice five times with each leg.
10. From a standing position holding the wand with one hand as it stands on end, take the hand off the wand, run around it and catch the wand before it falls. Complete five successful catches.
11. From a squatting position, grasp the wand at the ends, step forward over the wand, then step back again. Repeat five times in both directions.
12. From a squatting position holding the wand with both hands as it stands on end, turn the body around so the back faces the wand (180° turn). Complete the turn back to the starting position (360° total turn). Repeat two complete turns.
13. From a sitting position (knees bent, feet on the floor), place the

wand on the ankles and straighten the legs so the wand rises in the air and is caught with the hands. Repeat five times.

14. From a sitting position (knees bent), grasp the wand with both hands and place it under the feet. Bring the legs straight up and balance in a V-seat with the wand held under the legs. Hold the balance five seconds then release. Repeat five times.

15. Using music with a ¾ rhythm such as a waltz, combine four tasks from Tasks #1-#14 into a short sequence.

16. Repeat Task #15 using four different tasks.

17. Repeat Task #15 creating at least two wand movements not presented in Tasks #1-#14.

18. Combine a variety of wand movements to music to create a rhythmic routine. Concentrate on flowing smoothly from one wand movement to another and keeping in rhythm to the music.

19. Demonstrate the wand routine from Task #18 to the class attempting to perform with precision.

20. Perform the wand routine to music within a 40' × 40' area moving the body throughout the entire area during the routine. (These are some of the guidelines which qualify the routine for competition.)

(NOTE: Wands can be constructed by purchasing 1-inch diameter dowel rods and cutting them into 3-feet lengths.)

ELEVEN

Soccer

KICK—PASS

Purpose:
To advance the ball by passing to a teammate or to score.

Skill Analysis:
1. Focus eyes on the ball.
2. Keep arms free at sides for balance.
3. Contact the ball behind and below center.
4. Precede the kick with a step or two to impart additional force.
5. Kick with either foot.
6. Pass through open spaces and ahead of teammate.

Kinds: Inside of foot, outside of foot, toe, and heel.

Task Learning Experiences:
1. Kick into a wall target 10 times using each kind of kick (inside of foot, toe, outside of foot, and heel) from a stationary position.
2. Repeat Task #1 hitting the target five out of ten times with each kick.
3. Repeat Tasks #1 and #2 from a three step approach. Eliminate the heel pass.
4. From a stationary position, kick at a pin (use all kicks). Complete five out of ten, seven out of ten successful hits.
5. From a moving position, kick at a pin using inside of foot and toe. Complete five out of ten, seven out of ten successful hits.

6. In partners, kick to a stationary partner who is to your front, left side, right side, and behind five times. Use the appropriate kind of pass. Reverse.
7. In partners, A uses a toe lift kick to send the ball high over B's head five times. Reverse.
8. In partners while moving, combine a dribble and pass to a moving partner who is to your right, left, and diagonally ahead of you five times. Reverse.
9. In partners, complete five successful passes while moving at average speed across the width of the field.
10. In partners, complete five successful passes while moving at maximum speed across the width of the field.
11. While traveling down the center of the field, dribble and diagonally pass to the left alley five times.
12. While traveling down the center of the field, dribble and diagonally pass to the right alley five times.
13. While traveling down the left alley, dribble and diagonally pass to the right alley five times.
14. Dribble from 25-yard line and kick for goal. Score three consecutive goals. Kick from center, diagonal right, and diagonal left positions.
15. In partners, dribble and pass from 50-yard line and kick for goal. Complete successful passes and goal three out of five times.
16. In groups of three, A and B pass and dribble from the 50-yard line and kick for goal. C plays goalie and defends the goal. Complete successful passes and goal two out of five times, 3/5.
17. Repeat Task #16 and add another defensive player.
18. In groups of three, use triangular passing from 50-yard line and kick for goal.
19. Repeat Task #18 adding a goalie.
20. Repeat Task #18 adding two fullbacks and a goalie.

TRAP

Purpose:
To stop a rolling or bouncing ball.

Skill Analysis:
1. Align the body with oncoming ball.
2. Focus the eyes on the ball.
3. Incline the body forward.
4. Keep the arms free at sides for balance.
5. Apply force by catching the ball in a pocket formed by the body part and the ground.
6. Keep trapped ball within a step from the body.
7. Assume normal playing position as quickly as possible.

Kinds: Inside of lower leg, inside of both legs, front of both legs, and sole of foot.

Task Learning Experiences:
1. Kick the ball into the wall and trap rebound with the sole of the foot. Repeat until successful five consecutive times.
2. Kick the ball into the wall and trap rebound with the inside of the leg. Repeat until successful five consecutive times.
3. Kick the ball into wall and trap rebound with the inside of both legs or front of both legs. Repeat until successful five consecutive times.
4. In partners, A rolls the ball toward B and calls the kind of trap. B traps. Roll the ball 10 times. Reverse.
5. In partners, A bounces the ball toward B. B traps using inside of front of both legs. Repeat 10 times. Reverse.
6. Repeat Tasks #4 and 5 with the ball being rolled or bounced to both sides.
7. In partners, A kicks the ball toward B. B traps five times with inside of one leg. Other leg. Reverse.
8. Repeat Task #7 using inside of two legs or front of two legs.
9. Repeat Task #7 using the sole of foot trap.
10. In partners, A kicks the ball to right side of B. B traps and kicks the ball back to A who traps. Trap 10 balls using a variety of traps. Repeat to the left side.
11. Repeat Task #10 kicking to either side. Try to deceive your partner.

DRIBBLE

Purpose:
To maintain possession and to advance the ball.

Skill Analysis:
1. Tap ball lightly below the center.
2. Use both feet for dribbling.
3. Keep the ball one or two feet in front of the feet.
4. Keep the arms free for balance.
5. Focus the eyes on the ball while maintaining awareness of total situation.

Kinds: Inside of foot, outside of foot, toe.

Task Learning Experiences:
1. Dribble the width of the field three times using inside of foot dribble.
2. Repeat Task #1 using a zigzag pathway.
3. Dribble in a circular pathway using an inside of foot dribble.
4. Repeat Tasks #1, 2, and #3 using the outside of foot dribble.
5. Repeat Tasks #1, #2, and #3 using a toe dribble.

6. Dribble through Indian club obstacles using the inside of foot dribble.
7. Repeat Task #6 using a toe dribble.
8. Repeat Tasks #6 and #7 for time. Record the best time from two trials.
9. Combine inside and outside of foot dribbling in a circular pathway.
10. Dribble in a straight pathway and on signal (whistle) dribble in circular pathway combining inside and outside of foot dribbling.
11. Dribble in straight pathway and on signal (whistle) change direction or pathway.
12. Repeat Task #11 at full speed.
13. In partners and moving in the same direction, A dribbles 8-10 feet and passes diagonally ahead to B who dribbles and passes diagonally ahead to A. Continue the length of the soccer field and return so the passing is to the other side of the body.
14. In groups of three, repeat Task #13 adding a defensive player.

TACKLE

Purpose:
To take the ball away from the opponent.

Skill Analysis: Front Tackle
1. Tackle directly in front of oncoming opponent.
2. Flex the knees.
3. Distribute the weight evenly.
4. Incline the body forward.
5. Free arms at side for balance.
6. Focus the eyes on ball.
7. Reach and place a foot on the ball.
8. Shift the weight on back foot.
9. Avoid body contact with opponent.
10. Pass immediately.

Hook Tackle
1. Tackle in front and slightly to one side of oncoming opponent.
2. See Skills #2, #3, #4, #5, #6, and #9 for front tackle skills.
3. Extend nearest leg to opponent sideways with inside of foot toward ground.
4. Hook and pull the ball away.
5. Pass immediately.

Side Tackle
1. Tackle running parallel with the opponent — side by side position.

2. See Skills #2, #3, #4, #5, #6 and #9 for front tackle skills.
3. Use outside of foot and tap ball away from opponent or —
4. Run ahead and around opponent picking up the dribble when the ball is not in contact with the opponent's feet.
5. Continue to dribble or pass if Skill #4 is used.

Task Learning Experiences:

1. In partners and with one soccer or playground ball, play Keep Away in a 10 to 15-foot area for three minutes. Rules prohibit body contact and kicking the ball out of the designated area. Together discuss the techniques which were used to successfully maintain position of the ball or to take the ball away. Repeat Keep Away for another three minutes concentrating on the points of discussion.
2. In partners, A dribbles toward B who executes a front tackle. Walk through concentrating on the skill analysis. Reverse. Repeat three times.
3. Repeat Task #2 at half speed. Reverse. Repeat three times.
4. Repeat Task #2 at full speed. Reverse. Repeat three times.
5. In threes, A dribbles toward B who executes a front tackle and immediately passes to C. Walk through. Rotate. Repeat three times.
6. Repeat Task #5 increasing to half speed. Rotate. Repeat three times.
7. Repeat Task #5 increasing to full speed. Rotate. Repeat until each has successfully tackled and passed three times.
8. Repeat Tasks #2-#7 executing a hook tackle.
9. In partners, A dribbles while B moves alongside of A. B executes a side tackle and dribbles back toward the starting point. Walk through concentrating on mechanics. Reverse. Repeat three times.
10. Repeat Task #9 at half speed. Reverse. Repeat three times.
11. Repeat Task #9 at full speed. Reverse. Repeat three times.
12. In two teams of two each, Team A dribbles and passes toward opponents, Team B, who try to tackle executing a front or hook tackle. A marked neutral area can be used so that points can be awarded to the Team who moves the ball out of the neutral zone. Play continues until one team scores a predetermined number of points or for a set time period.
13. A forward line of five offensive players dribble and pass against five defensive players positioned as halfbacks and fullbacks. Points are scored when the offensive line advances the ball to a designated area or to the defensive team if they tackle and advance the ball to a designated area in the opposite direction. Play continues until a set number of points are scored or for a set time period.

VOLLEY

Purpose:
To redirect an aerial ball strategically.

Skill Analysis:
1. Align body part with approaching ball.
2. Focus the eyes on approaching ball.
3. Move total body and body part toward ball.
4. Apply firm body part to center of the ball.
5. Follow through toward intended flight direction.

   Kinds: Foot, knee, shoulder, and head.

Task Learning Experiences:
1. In partners, A throws the ball toward B's shoulder and B volleys the ball executing a shoulder volley. Repeat five times from a distance of 10 feet. Reverse. Repeat from 15 feet.
2. Repeat Task #1 preceding the volley with two or three steps. Reverse.
3. Repeat Tasks #1 and #2 directing the ball to the left, right, and toward center.
4. Repeat Tasks #1, #2, and #3 executing a knee volley.
5. Repeat Tasks #1, #2, and #3 executing a foot volley.
6. In partners, A throws the ball underhand so that it arches and drops toward B's head. B executes a head volley. Repeat three times from a distance of 10 feet. Reverse.
7. Repeat Task #6 directing the ball to the left, right, and toward center.
8. Stand 10 to 15 feet from a wall and kick the ball into the wall. Volley the rebound with different body parts according to the level of rebound. For a more forceful rebound, precede the kick with two or three steps. Different levels of rebound can be achieved by contacting the ball at various points below the center. Repeat 10 times.

BLOCK

Purpose:
To stop the progress of an aerial ball.

Skill Analysis:
1. Align the body part with approaching ball.
2. Focus the eyes on approaching ball.
3. Relax or collapse the body part which contacts the ball to absorb the oncoming force.
4. Recover and pass.

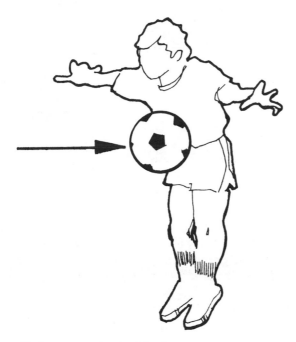

Abdomen or body block

inside of leg and thigh and foot.

Task Learning Experiences:
1. Repeat volley Tasks #1, #2, and #8 substituting the body parts listed for blocking.
2. In partners and from a distance of 10-15 feet, A lifts the ball while passing to B who uses different body parts to block the ball. Reverse and repeat 10 times. Concentrate on blocking the ball and dropping it within a foot or two of the body.
3. In groups of three, repeat Task #2 with B passing quickly to C. Rotate and repeat 10 times.

PUNT AND DROP KICK

Purpose:
To clear the ball away from the goal area (used only by the goal keeper.)

Skill Analysis:
1. Spread fingers holding the ball in front of the body.
2. Flex the elbows slightly.
3. Position feet together.
4. Incline body slightly forward.

5. Focus the eyes on the ball.
6. Step forward on the left foot as the ball is dropped.
7. Contact the ball on top of the instep.
8. Contact the ball directly from a drop—punt.
9. Contact the ball after rebounding from the ground—drop kick.
10. Follow through in direction of intended flight.

Task Learning Experiences:
1. Punt five balls concentrating on the skills analysis.
2. Punt five balls from a stationary position.
3. Punt five balls from a moving position. Use one or two steps.
4. Punt three balls a minimum of 20 yards.
5. Punt three balls a minimum of 30 yards.
6. From a goalie's position, punt three balls toward the left alley. Repeat toward the right alley and down the center.
7. In partners, A kicks the ball toward B who picks the ball up and punts. Concentrate on getting the punt away quickly. Repeat 10 times and reverse.
8. Repeat Task #7 punting toward the left alley, the right alley.
9. Repeat Tasks #1-#8 using a drop kick.

TWELVE

Softball

THROW AND CATCH

Purpose (Throw):
To put a batter or baserunner out and to prevent advancement of baserunners and scoring.

Purpose (Catch):
To catch hit or thrown balls in order to put a batter or baserunner out and to prevent advancement of baserunners and scoring.

Skill Analysis:
See analysis for Overhand Throw and Catch in the chapter on Selected Fundamental Skills.

Additional Skill Analysis:
Sidearm or Underarm Whip
1. Plant feet in forward stride fielding position.
2. Grip with the thumbs on top, first two fingers on the side and the other two fingers supporting under the ball.
3. Swing the arm back below the shoulder parallel with ground.
4. Extend the forearm and cock the wrist.
5. Swing the arm forward across the body.
6. Transfer the weight forward and swing the arm forward about waist high.
7. Release by snapping the wrist.
8. Follow through in front of body in direction of intended flight.

Task Learning Experiences:

1. In partners, A stands in an area about 20 feet from a wall and throws overhand against the wall. B observes A's throwing form according to overhand throwing mechanics. Throw five balls and reverse. Increase the distance.
2. Throw (overhand) at a wall target from 20 feet. Repeat until successful five out of ten, seven out of ten times.
3. Repeat Task #2 by increasing the distance.
4. Repeat Task #2 by decreasing the size of the target.
5. In partners, A and B throw and catch from a distance of 25 feet. Concentrate on good throwing form. Continue for five minutes.
6. Repeat Task #5 by successfully completing 20 consecutive errorless throws and catches.
7. Repeat Task #5 by varying the amount of force applied to each throw.
8. Repeat Tasks #5, #6, and #7 by increasing the distance.
9. In partners, A throws grounders to B who fields and throws to A using a sidearm throw. Throw five balls and reverse. Repeat for five trials each.
10. Repeat Tasks #5, #6, #7, and #8 using a sidearm throw.
11. In groups of four and in a square formation, A throws to B who catches and throws to C and C to D, D to A. Concentrate on catching and quickly releasing the ball. Continue for five minutes. Use both overhand and sidearm throws.

12. Repeat Task #11 by completing five trips around without an error. Repeat by completing five consecutive errorless trips.
13. Repeat Tasks #11 and #12 on a regular diamond.
14. Repeat Task #11 on a diamond by tagging the bag after each catch. Reverse directions. Concentrate on combining catching and tagging into one movement and quickly getting into throwing position.
15. Repeat Tasks #11 and #14 on a diamond, time three errorless trips and record the best.
16. In groups of three, throw for distance. Take five trials. Measure and record only the longest. A throws, B marks and C retrieves. Rotate.
17. In partners and about 40 feet apart, A rolls soft grounders toward B who quickly runs forward, scoops the ball and tosses underhand to A. Repeat five times and reverse.
18. In groups of three, A throws grounders (or bats from a tee) to B and C who are positioned on each side and about 15-20 feet from a base. Practice fielding the ball and tossing underhand to the other who will run to cover the base. Mix the direction of ground balls. Rotate after throwing 10 balls.

BAT

Purpose:
To reach base safely, to advance baserunners and to score runs.

Skill Analysis:
1. Grip: Hold bat firmly (end, standard, choke grip).
2. Stance: Place feet about shoulder width apart (open, square, closed stance).
3. Flex knees slightly.
4. Hold bat up and to right of right shoulder.
5. Turn head toward pitcher.
6. Focus on oncoming ball.
7. Rotate hips to right shifting weight over back foot.
8. Swing forward, rotating hips followed by arms and hands.
9. Shift weight forward keeping hips and shoulders level.
10. Roll wrists after contact (or miss).
11. Follow through with full swing.

Task Learning Experiences:
1. Swing the bat 8-10 times concentrating on the mechanics of batting.
2. In partners, repeat Task #1. A swings the bat while B checks performance. Reverse.
3. Hit a suspended ball 10 times. Concentrate on smooth and balanced swing, shifting weight evenly, and follow through.
4. Repeat Task #3 at variable ball heights.
5. From a batting tee, hit the ball for distance. Repeat 10 times.
6. From a batting tee, hit the ball on different surface points several times. What flight pattern did you notice?
7. From a batting tee, hit several balls while taking an open stance, closed stance, square stance. What flight patterns did you notice?
8. From a batting tee, hit several balls from a forward batting box position and a deep batting box position. What flight patterns did you notice?
9. From a batting tee, hit five balls to the left side, five to the center and five to the right side. What adjustments did you make?
10. From a batting tee placed on home plate, hit five consecutive balls on the fly into the outfield.
11. In groups of four, A pitches, B bats, C and D field. Hit five balls and rotate.
12. Repeat Task #11 hitting three out of five ground balls.
13. Repeat Task #11 hitting 3/5 fly balls.
14. Repeat Task #11 hitting 3/5 line drives.
15. Repeat Task #11 hitting 3/5 balls to the left side.
16. Repeat Task #11 hitting 3/5 balls to the right side.

17. Repeat Task #11 hitting 3/5 balls down the center.
18. Repeat Task #11 hitting 3/5 balls 100 feet, 125 feet, 150 feet on the fly.
19. Self-toss and bat the ball for distance. (A whiffle set could be used for smaller and younger students.)
20. Self-toss and bat the ball for flies, grounders, and placement.
21. In groups of five or six, A pitches, B bats, C catches, rest play field. Batter practices hitting and rapid start to first base. Repeat 5 times and rotate.
22. Repeat Task #21 but time the run to first base. Record fastest time for each player.
23. In groups of five, six or seven, repeat Tasks #11-#17 on a regular diamond.
24. In partners, explain in writing:
    24.1   How do you hit a ball to the third base side of the diamond?
    24.2   How do you hit a ball to the first base side of the diamond?
    24.3   How do you hit a ball through the center of the diamond?
    Get a bat and ball and test your answers.

BUNT

Purpose:

Skill Analysis:
Stance
1. Pivot (from normal stance) on ball of left foot.
2. Step right, parallel to plate.
3. Square body to face the pitcher.
4. Spread feet apart with more weight on right foot.

Grip
1. Keep bottom hand on top of bat.
2. Grip with forefinger and thumb.
3. Slide top hand up behind the trademark.
4. Rest bat on loosely clenched fist with thumb behind the bat.

Action
1. Begin bunt position when ball is about to be released.
2. Combine grip and stance into one movement.
3. Keep eye on oncoming ball.
4. Maintain a loose grip to absorb the force of the ball.
5. Lay (do not swing) the bat on the ball.
6. Angle the bat downward on the ball to left, center, right.

Kinds: drag, push.

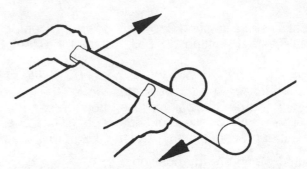

Hand position for bunting grip

Task Learning Experiences:

1. In partners, A shows the grip and bat position for the bunt and B checks. Reverse.
2. In partners, A shows the pivot and stance for the bunt and B checks. Reverse.
3. In partners, A combines grip and stance into one movement from a normal batting stance five times. B checks. Reverse.
4. Repeat Task #3, with A moving into bunting position on a signal from B. Repeat five times and reverse.
5. Using a batting tee, repeat Task #4 concentrating on pushing the ball on a downward angle. Reverse.
6. In partners, A pitches the ball from a short distance to B who is in a bunt position (regular balls and bats or whiffle sets can be used). Bunt 10 times hitting only those balls in the strike zone. Reverse.
7. Repeat Task #6 with B beginning from a normal batting stance and increasing the pitching distance. Reverse.
8. Repeat Task #7 by directing the ball to the left or down an imaginary third base line.
9. Repeat Task #7 by directing the ball to center or toward the pitcher.
10. Repeat Task #7 by directing the ball to the right or down an imaginary first base line.
11. In groups of five, A plays first base, B plays third base, C pitches, D catches and E bats. The batter bunts and runs to first. Defensive players try to put the batter out. Rotate until all have had five trials.
12. In groups of seven, A plays first, B second, C third, D pitches, E catches, F is a runner on first, G bats. The batter bunts and defense tries to put the runner out at second. Rotate until all have had five trials.
13. Combine Task #12 into a game whereby the defense scores a point if they can put out the runner at second base. The offense scores a point if the runner reaches second base safely. Defensive players must begin from normal fielding positions.

FIELDING

Purpose:
To catch a ball, to stop a ball and/or throw a ball in order to put a batter out or to prevent the advancement of runners or scoring.

Skill Analysis:
General Fielding
1. Assume waiting ready position.
    1.1 Feet comfortably apart
    1.2 Weight over balls of feet.
    1.3 Knees flexed.
    1.4 Mentally know next play if ball comes to you.
2. Move quickly when ball is hit.
    2.1 Move forward to meet balls in front.
    2.2 Move diagonally forward or backward for balls on either side.
    2.3 Turn and run on fly balls hit deeply behind.
3. Keep eyes on oncoming ball.
4. Point fingers downward, little fingers together for balls below waist.
5. Point fingers upward, thumbs together for ball above waist.
6. Position feet in left forward strike to aid throw.

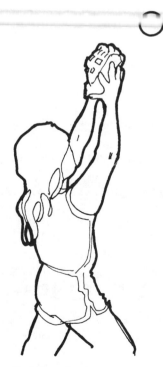

Fielding fly balls

Fielding ground balls

7. Absorb the force by "giving" in direction of the backswing for a throw.
8. Begin to grip for a throw immediately upon catching.
9. Complete the next play quickly.

Additional Skill Analysis:
Fly Balls
1. Look over shoulder when moving sideways or backward.
2. Catch ball high and, if possible, on throwing side.

Task Learning Experiences:
1. Throw the ball upward and catch several times. Concentrate on catching ball close to right shoulder, absorbing force and keeping eyes on ball.
2. Repeat Task #1 by throwing slightly to left and right and move to catching position.
3. Repeat Task #1 by throwing ahead and behind and move to catching position.
4. In partners, A throws high balls to B who returns high balls to A. Each catch five balls.
5. Repeat Task #4 by throwing to the right side. Catch five balls.
6. Repeat Task #4 by throwing to the left side.
7. Repeat Task #4 by throwing in front of partner.
8. Repeat Task #4 by throwing behind partner.
9. In groups of three, A hits flies to B and C. Catch five balls and rotate batter.
10. In groups of three, A bats or throws fly balls to B who catches and quickly throws to C who is close to A. (Simulate throw to home plate).
11. Repeat Task #10 with C about halfway between batter and fielder. (Simulate relay throw).

12. On a diamond and in groups of five, A bats fly balls to outfielders B, C, and D who catch and quickly throw to E at home plate. Rotate.
13. Repeat Task #12 with E on second base.
14. Repeat Task #12 and add a runner on third base who tries to score after the catch.

Additional Skill Analysis:
Ground Balls
1. Move to meet oncoming balls.
2. Flex knees and keep weight low.
3. Scoop ball with glove hand and trap with throwing hand.

Task Learning Experiences:
1. Throw a tennis ball against a wall and field the rebound. Concentrate on moving to meet the ball and keeping the eyes focused on the oncoming ball.
2. Repeat Task #1 by throwing with varying amounts of force. Field 20 balls cleanly.
3. Repeat Tasks #1 and #2 by angling the throw for angled rebounds. Concentrate on maneuverability and footwork.
4. In partners, A throws ground ball to B who fields and throws a grounder back to A. Field 10 balls cleanly.
5. Repeat Task #4 by throwing to right side of partner.
6. Repeat Task #4 by throwing to left side of partner.
7. Repeat Task #4 by alternating throwing directions and varying the amount of force.
8. Repeat Tasks #4, #5, #6, and #7 with A throwing grounders to B who fields the ball and quickly throws back to A. After fielding and throwing 10 errorless times, reverse.
9. In groups of three, A throws grounders to B who fields and quickly throws to C who is in a simulated first base position. Field five balls and rotate.
10. Repeat Task #9 with A batting self-tossed balls or hitting from a tee.
11. Repeat Task #10 by alternating directions and varying the force of the hit ball.
12. Repeat Task #10 with C positioned at home plate.
13. In groups of five and on a diamond, A bats self-tossed balls or hits from a tee, B and C are fielders in area of short stop and second base, D plays first base, E stands on home plate and runs to first base on each hit ball. B and C attempt to throw the runner out. Hit five balls and rotate.
14. Repeat Task #13 by adding scoring. Thrower scores a point when the runner is thrown out and the runner scores a point when the runner beats the throw to first. Rotate position after each hit. Continue until a player reaches five points.

PITCH

Purpose:
To put the ball in play by throwing it underhand so that it travels through or near the strike zone in such a manner that the batter will have difficulty hitting it.

Skill Analysis:
Grip
    1. Hold the ball with the thumb and three fingers over the seam with the little finger on the side for support.
    2. For larger hands, hold the ball in a tripod grip with the thumb and first two finger pads over the seam.
    3. Do not let the ball rest in the palm.

Rules
    1. Stand with both feet about shoulder width apart on the plate facing the batter.
    2. Hold ball with both hands.
    3. Remain in position 1-20 seconds.
    4. Release below the hip with wrist no further from body than elbow.

Straight Pitch
    1. Focus eyes on catcher's target.
    2. Extend both hands forward.

3. Bring throwing arm down and back in an arc.
4. Rotate body slightly toward pitching arm.
5. Cock wrist at end of backswing.
6. Start motion by rotating body forward.
7. Swing arm downward and forward.
8. Carry body momentum forward with a step on left foot.
9. Release the ball just forward of the body.
10. Roll ball off fingertips.
11. Follow through with the arm moving upward.
12. Step forward with right foot.
13. Assume ready fielding position.

Task Learning Experiences:

1. From a distance of about 20 feet, pitch the ball into a wall for five minutes. Concentrate on the mechanics and rules of pitching.
2. In partners, repeat Task #1 so that A observes and checks the pitching performance of B. Reverse.
3. In partners, A pitches to B who catches and returns to A. Start about 20 feet apart.
4. Repeat Task #3 and add a home plate or a similar marker. Repeat until each can successfully place 15 pitched balls over the plate.
5. Repeat Task #4 by increasing the distance to 25 feet, 30 feet (35 feet and 40 feet optional or for pitching specialists).
6. Pitch into a wall target from 20 feet and successfully score five out of ten, 7/10, 9/10 pitches.
7. Repeat Task #6 from 25 feet, 30 feet (35 and 40 feet optional or for pitching specialists).
8. In partners, repeat Tasks #6 and #7 with A pitching 10 balls and B standing in batting position. No hitting. Reverse.
9. Repeat Task #8 by counting balls and strikes. (A strike crosses home plate between the top of the knees and arm pits of the batter).
10. In partners, A pitches and B stands in batting box. No hitting. A remains pitching until 10 consecutive strikes are pitched. Reverse.
11. In groups of five, A pitches, B catches, C bats, D and E field. Rotate after each pitches for three minutes or 10 balls.
12. In partners, A pitches and B bunts. After each bunt, the pitcher fields the bunt as quickly as possible. Reverse three times after alternating trials of five pitches each.
13. Pitch two innings of game play.

THIRTEEN

Tennis

FOREHAND DRIVE

Purpose:
To return balls that are received on the racket side of the body.

Skill Analysis:
1. Grip—shake hands with the racket so that "V" formed by thumb and forefinger is centrally located on the top of the grip.
2. Backswing early and transfer weight over the back foot.
3. Keep racket head above wrist.
4. Flex the knees—body torso straight.
5. Rotate body weight forward with the swing.
6. Lock the wrist and hold with a firm grip.
7. Stroke flat—rising slowly at contact.
8. Contact ball ahead of torso.
9. Keep eyes on contact point a split second after contact.
10. Swing through parallel to net as long as possible.

Task Learning Experiences:
1. Stand sideways to wall, backboard, or fence and hit 10 dropped balls with open palm of hand. Concentrate on transferring the weight over the back foot on the backswing and forward and into the ball on the forward swing.
2. Repeat Task #1 using tennis racket.

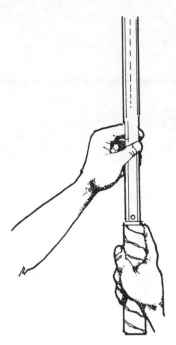

Forehand tennis grip

3. Use forehand stroke and hit into wall, fence, or backboard. After each hit come to ready position. Complete five, 10, 15 consecutive hits.
4. Repeat Task #3 but tape or hang a target and aim for the target. Complete three out of ten, five out of ten, or seven out of ten target hits.
5   Stand between baseline and service center line and drop and hit 10 legal (within bounds) forehand drives to the opposite side.
6. Repeat Task #5 but place 10 legal drives into opposite back court area.
7. Repeat Task #5 but place five legal drives down the left side and five legal drives down the right side of the opposite court.
8. In partners, A tosses from a position near the net to the forehand side while B hits three out of ten, five out of ten, or seven of ten legal drives across net.
9. Repeat Task #8 with A tossing the ball to different forehand areas so B must move forward, backward, side and diagonally forward and backward. Stress: move—stop—hit.
10. Repeat Task #8 but designate target areas to hit into.
11. Repeat Task #8 but throw ball with more force.
12. Rally with a partner using forehand drives.
13. In partners, each stands inside the service court on opposite sides of the net and returns 10, 15, 20 consecutive hits into the service court from the forehand side. Remember to stress racket control by gently stroking.

14. Repeat Task #13 but stand between baseline and service court line. The ball must be contacted in this area even if it bounces more than once.
15. Repeat Task #13 but stand behind the baseline. Do not step inside the court area to hit. Let the ball bounce more than once if necessary. Concentrate on force.
16. In groups of six, use a shuttle formation with three on each side of the net. After every forehand hit go to the end of the line. Count the total legal returns in a given time period or score total consecutive legal hits for each set of three.

BACKHAND DRIVE

Purpose:
To return balls that are received on the nonracket side of the body.

Skill Analysis:
1. Grip—rotate racket from forehand grip so "V" of thumb and forefinger is on the top level. Spread fingers slightly.
2. Backswing straight carrying nonracket hand into backswing and release.
3. Rotate the weight over the back foot.
4. [illegible]
5. Rotate body weight forward with the swing.
6. Stroke level rising slightly.

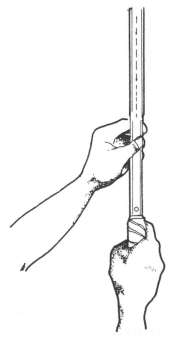

Backhand tennis grip

7. Lock the wrist and hold with a firm grip.
8. Contact ball ahead of forward foot.
9. Keep eye contact point a split second after contact.
10. Swing through toward net with racket ending slightly above shoulders.

Task Learning Exeriences:

1. Stand sideways to wall, backboard, or fence and hit 10 dropped balls. The ball is tossed up from left hand so that it drops ahead of right foot. Concentrate on shifting weight back, swinging, and stepping.
2. Repeat Task #1 finishing with a ready position.
3. In partners, A tosses 10 balls to backhand side and B hits backhand drive into wall or fence. Reverse.
4. Repeat Task #3 on a court with the tossing partner standing near the net and throwing to the backhand side of the partner who is positioned in "no man's land" (area between the service and baseline). Stress the return to ready position after each hit. Reverse.
5. Repeat Task #4 legally returning three out of ten, five out of ten, or seven out of ten backhand drives.
6. Repeat Task #4 but A throws to different court areas so B will have to move forward, backward, sideways and diagonally forward and backward.
7. Repeat Task #4 with hitting partner a step behind the baseline. Reverse.
8. Repeat Task #7 legally returning three out of ten, 5/10, or 7/10 backhand drives.
9. In threes, A stands in service court area and throws five balls to B who returns a backhand legally, C retrieves. Rotate positions. Individual or team scores can be kept or a set number of legal returns can be required for individuals or the group. The group can be expanded to four or five.
10. In partners, rally concentrating on hitting as many balls as possible with a backhand drive.
11. In partners, each stands inside the service court on opposite sides of the net and using the backhand only, returns 10, 15, 20 consecutive hits into the service court area. Remember to stress racket control by gently stroking.
12. Repeat Task #11 but stand in no man's land. The ball must be contacted in this area even if it bounces more than one time. More force will be needed.
13. Repeat Task #11 from a position behind the baseline. Concentrate on force.
14. In partners, rally for five minutes from the back area of the court using both forehand and backhand drives. Concentrate on legal returns and returning to "home base" which is just behind the center mark of the baseline.

SERVE (FLAT)

Purpose:
To put the ball into play by sending the ball over the net and into the diagonal court.

Skill Analysis:
1. Grip about halfway between forehand and backhand.
2. Stand with hip and shoulder sideways to net.
3. Toss ball straight upward with no spin.
4. Start ball hand and racket downward together.
5. Swing racket hand away and behind body.
6. Lift the ball hand upward and toss the ball.
7. Move racket up behind the back.
8. Lead with the elbow as racket is swung upward and forward.
9. Shift weight upward and forward with racket.

See serving task #5

Tennis Serve

10. Contact with a full extension of racket arm.
11. Follow through in direction of serve.

Kinds: Slice and Twist.

Task Learning Experiences:

1. Toss ball up and let it drop to the ground 10 times. Remove the spin by tossing with the thumb and first two fingers.
2. Toss about 4-8 inches above the extended racket head and let ball drop slightly to the right and just in front of the left foot.
3. Start the serve with the racket behind the back (back scratching position) and weight on the back foot. Toss the ball up and meet the ball at extended racket point. Repeat 10 times. Do not hit the ball—toss, meet, and stop.
4. Starting the serve with the racket behind the back, toss ball and serve into the fence or wall 10 times. Use a line for feet placement and rules. The court baseline makes a good line for fence practice.
5. Repeat Task #4 serving from the service court line on a court. Change from the right side to the left side.
6. Repeat Task #5 legally serving five out of ten or seven out of ten balls.
7. Repeat Task #5 moving to the baseline.
8. Repeat Task #7 legally serving three out of ten, five out of ten, or seven out of ten.

9. Coordinate toss and full swing. Serve ball into backboard, wall, or fence 10 times.
10. Repeat Task #9 adding a serving line so the serve can be practiced with rules.
11. Serve 10 legal serves from the right side using the full swing from the service court line.
12. Serve 10 legal serves from the left side using the full swing from the service court line.
13. Repeat Task #11 from behind the right baseline.
14. Repeat Task #12 from the left baseline.
15. Repeat Tasks #13 and #14 placing the serves near the center line.
16. Repeat Tasks #13 and #14 placing the serve near the side court line.

VOLLEY

Purpose:
To hit the ball before it bounces in order to gain an offensive advantage.

Skill Analysis:
1. Grip for a forehand or backhand.
2. Open racket face on both sides (ready position).
3. Backswing to the shoulder for either side.
4. Maintain firm wrist throughout.
5. Step into stroke for more force.
6. Contact the ball in front of body.
7. Direct the racket head downward.
8. Finish the stroke barely beyond contact point.

Task Learning Experience:
1. In partners, A throws 10 balls toward B's right shoulder. B grips the racket by the shaft and uses a forehand volley directing the ball downward at A's feet. Concentrate on keeping the backswing and forehand swing as short as possible. Reverse.
2. Repeat Task #1 holding the racket by the grip.
3. Repeat Tasks #1 and #2 using a backhand volley with A throwing toward B's left shoulder.
4. In partners, A throws 10 balls to B who is positioned near the net on a court. B volleys forehand and backhand. Reverse.
5. Repeat Task #4 aiming for thrower's feet.
6. Repeat Task #4 aiming for sharp angle placements to the left or right side of the court.
7. Repeat Task #4 aiming toward the deep corners.
8. In groups of three, A hits 10 balls from the baseline to B and C who are positioned near the net. B or C returns forehand and backhand volleys. Rotate.

9. Repeat Task #8 aiming for sharp angle placements to the left and right side of the court.
10. Repeat Task #8 aiming toward the deep corners.
11. In groups of four, repeat Task #8 with D positioned in the forecourt as a partner of A. B and C aim the volley at D's feet or at sharp angles away from D. D attempts to return the volley. Add a scoring element for more interest.
12. In partners and deep in court position, A hits a groundstroke deep to B who returns the stroke and follows the stroke to the net and tries to volley A's return. Repeat 10 times starting from original position after the rally ends. Rotate.
13. In partners, volley rally in forecourt. Try to keep rally going as long as possible.

LOB

Purpose:
To send the opponent deep when he is near the net (offensive) and to allow time for the player who has been forced out of position to regain a more favorable court position (defensive).

Skill Analysis:
1. Use a grip, stance, beginning swing, and point of contact that are similar to the drives (groundstrokes).
2. Shorten the backswing.
3. Open the racket face.
4. Loft the ball in a high arc.
5. Carry forward swing in an upward plane.
6. Use less force than for a groundstroke.

Task Learning Experience:
1. Drop 10 balls and hit using a lob. Concentrate on the amount of force used, the racket face angle, and the descent of the ball.
2. Go to a court, stand in no man's land and drop 10 balls. Lob to back area of opposite court.
3. Repeat Task #2 but lob from different areas of the court.
4. In partners, A stands in the middle of the service court area and throws to the forehand side of B who lobs over the head of A. Throw five balls and reverse.
5. Repeat Task #4 making two out of five legal lobs, 3/5, or 4/5.
6. Repeat Tasks #4 and #5 with backhand lobs. (Note that Tasks #4, #5, and #6 can be done in groups of three with C retrieving.)
7. In partners, A serves five balls to B who returns all serves with a lob. Reverse.
8. Rally 10 minutes mixing groundstrokes with lobs.
9. In groups of three with two or three groups per court, A stands in service court area and throws five balls to B who lobs over the

head of A. C retrieves. Score one point if the lob goes over A's head and lands in no man's land. Rotate. Scores can be individual or team. The group can be expanded to four or five.

NOTE: Similar tasks can be developed for advanced players using marked target areas and ball spin.

SMASH (OVERHEAD)

Purpose:
To produce a forceful stroke which will be unreturnable.

Skill Analysis:
1. Move to a position under and back of the ball.
2. Focus eyes on the ball.
3. Shift weight to back foot.
4. Aim nonracket hand toward ball.
5. Rotate body upward and forward.
6. Contact ball about a foot in front of the head at racket reach.
7. Contact and follow through in direction of intended flight.
8. Stroke forward and downward. Adjust according to distance from the net.

Task Learning Experiences:
1. In partners, A tosses high lobs to B who moves under and behind the ball and catches the ball above and to the right of the head. This is good for young beginners who need to concentrate on looking at the ball and getting into position. Reverse.
2. Stand 10 feet from the fence and self-toss 10 balls high. Use a smash stroke concentrating on timing.
3. Repeat Task #2 moving to a forecourt position.
4. In partners, A tosses high lobs to B who smashes. Concentrate on a forceful stroke directed in a downward flight. Reverse after 10 tosses.
5. Repeat Task #4 on a court with B positioned in the forecourt and A tossing from a sitting position close to the net to avoid being hit. Reverse.
6. Repeat Task #5 with A tossing to different forecourt position. Reverse.
7. Repeat Task #5 with B smashing to different court areas.
8. In partners, A hits lob and B smashes. Reverse after each has legally returned five smashes.
9. In partners, lob and smash. Practice smashing to different court areas.

FOURTEEN

Track and Field

SPRINT

Purpose:
To run a short distance in the fastest time possible.

Skill Analysis:
1. Assume a crouch start placing the stronger leg in front block and the rear leg knee opposite the heel of the front foot. (To set your marks).
2. Transfer weight slightly ahead of the hands. (Set.)
3. Push off with short driving steps as the arms move quickly in opposition to the legs. (Acceleration).
4. Keep the body at a low angle for approximately ten yards after the runner leaves the blocks to avoid loss of power.
5. Spring using high knee action and land on the balls of the feet while leaning the body forward slightly (20°-25° angle.)
6. Continue to move arms vigorously in opposition to the legs.
7. Spring across the finish line at maximum speed by imagining the finish line to be ten yards farther. This eliminates a premature decrease in speed.

Task Learning Experiences:
1. Run 25 yards concentrating on lifting the knees high.
2. Run 25 yards concentrating on taking long strides while using high knee action.
3. Run 25 yards concentrating on landing on the balls of the feet while using high knee action and long strides.

4. Run 25 yards concentrating on leaning forward while using high knee action, long strides, and landing on the balls of the feet.
5. Run 25 yards concentrating on strong use of the arms in opposition to the legs while using high knee action, long strides, a forward lean, and landing on the balls of the feet.
6. Repeat Task #5 with a partner attempting to cross a finish line at maximum speed.
7. Place body in a crouch start position:
   7.1 Fingertips behind the starting line forming an upside down "V" with the thumb and fingers.
   7.2 Stronger leg placed in front block with rear knee placed opposite heel of front foot. (If blocks are not available, brace against another student's feet.)
   7.3 Look ahead about 4-5 feet.
8. Stand up and again resume the crouch start position. Repeat 10 times.
9. Resume crouch start position and follow it with the "set" position. For the "set" position, raise hips which will lift the rear knee off the ground. Transfer body weight slightly ahead of the hands. Hold the "set" position very still to avoid a false start. Repeat five times.
10. Repeat the crouch start position, set position, and follow with the acceleration (go) for 25 yards. For the acceleration, initially use short driving steps starting with the rear foot, strong opposition arm movement, and a low body angle. An upright position should not be reached for at least ten yards.
11. In partners, A assumes the crouch start while B gives the commands (to your mark, set, go). A takes a 25-yard acceleration. Repeat three times and reverse.
12. In groups of four, combine the crouch start with a 25-yard acceleration. Repeat three times and record each trial. A is the sprinter, B evaluates the crouch start and acceleration, C times and records, and D gives the commands. Rotate positions.
13. Combine the entire crouch start and acceleration with the running technique which was practiced in Tasks #5 and #6. Sprint 50 yards.
14. In groups of three, repeat Task #13 with A sprinting, B giving commands, and C timing. Record the best of three trials and rotate.
15. Repeat Task #13 racing against one or several other students. Never look to the side to see the other students' progress. Look straight ahead.
16. Repeat Task #15 recording the times.
17. Repeat Tasks #13-#16 sprinting 75 yards. Sprinting 100 yards. Sprinting 220 yards.

NOTE: The teacher can establish standard times according to age and experience.

DISTANCE RUN

Purpose:

To run a distance of 880 yards or longer with the purpose of achieving maximum speed and endurance. (For upper elementary, the 440 yard run should be incorporated as a distance run.)

Skill Analysis:

1. Use a standard start in a forward-backward stride. (Only "set" and "go" commands are given.)
2. Take long strides, less height in knee action, and decrease body lean.
3. Relax while running to improve endurance.
4. Land on the ball of the foot, drop to the heel, and then push forward from the toes (rocking motion.)
5. Inhale through the nose and exhale through the mouth.

Task Learning Experiences:

1. Session One:
   1.1 Perform calisthenic warm-ups of total body with emphasis on feet (toes), ankles, calves.
   1.2 Run ¼ of the distance of the event.
   1.3 Spring 100 yards — walk 100 yards (rest), for a total of five times (interval training).
   1.4 Walk 440 yards to cool down.
2. Session Two:
   2.1 Perform calisthenics with emphasis on strength.
   2.2 Run ½ of distance of the event.
   2.3 Spring 220 yards — walk 220 yards (rest or recovery). Repeat three times.
   2.4 Jog 440 yards to cool down.
3. Session Three:
   3.1 Jog 880 yards as warm-up.
   3.2 Sprint 220 yards—jog 220 yards (recovery). Repeat four times.
   3.3 Jog 440 yards to cool down.
4. Session Four:
   4.1 Calisthenic warm-up—emphasize leg and arm flexibility.
   4.2 Run entire distance of the event at ½ speed.
   4.3 Jog 440 yards to cool down.
5. Session Five:
   5.1 Jog 440 yards for warm-up.
   5.2 Run twice the distance of the event at ½ speed.
   5.3 Walk 440 yards to cool down.
6. Session Six:
   6.1 Warm up with strength exercises.
   6.2 Run entire distance of event at ¾ speed.
   6.3 Cool down with 440-yard jog.

7. Session Seven:
   7.1 Jog 880 yards for warm-up.
   7.2 Spring 220 yards—jog 220 yards—repeat five times.
   7.3 Walk 440 yards to cool down.
8. Session Eight:
   8.1 Warm up with flexibility exercises.
   8.2 Run entire distance of event at full speed.
   8.3 Walk 440 yards to cool down.
9. Session Nine:
   9.1 Calisthenics—for strength.
   9.2 Run 2½ times the distance of the event, alternating sustained bursts of speed with jogging (Fartlek—speed play).
   9.3 Walk 440 yards to cool down.
10. Session Ten:
   10.1 Jog 440 yards as warm-up.
   10.2 Run entire distance of event for time.
   10.3 Cool down with 440-yard jog.
11. Session Eleven:
   11.1 Warm up with flexibility calisthenics and 440-yard jog.
   11.2 Run entire distance of event against opponent's in order to be aware of pacing self. Use either front runner or positional runner strategy. Front runner—sets pace for others. Positional runner—lets others set pace, passes in last 220 yards.
   11.3 Cool down with 44-yard walk.
12. Time and record the 440-yard run. The 880-yard run. The mile run.

NOTE: The teacher can establish standard times according to age and experience.

RELAYS

Purpose:
To perform a track event that involves a team effort of four individuals in which each team member runs a specified distance.

Skill Analysis: Shuttle Relay
1. Stand at opposite ends of a straightaway (two team members at each end).
2. Run only one leg of the race (from one line to the adjacent line).
3. Touch the right shoulder of the next runner as a signal for starting the next leg of the race.

Skill Analysis: Pursuit Relay
1. Pass a baton within a 22-yard passing zone to the next runner who is running in the same direction and in the same lane as the other team members.

2. Arrange the order of runners on a team so that the fastest student is last, the second fastest is first, the third fastest is third, and the slowest is second (two, four, three, one).
3. Hold the baton in the left hand and exchange to the right hand of the receiver. (A right-to-left exchange can be used.) After the exchange, the baton is placed into the left hand for the next passer to receive the exchange.
4. Use one of the following baton passes:
    4.1 Visual Pass—The receiver extends the arm to the rear with the palm turned downward. The receiver's eyes are kept on the baton until it is grasped. The passer brings the baton from underneath into the palm.
    4.2 Nonvisual Pass—The receiver forms a "V" with the receiving fingers and thumb so that the passer can bring the baton from underneath into the "V". The receiver does not turn to see the baton but accepts it looking straight ahead.

Task Learning Experiences:
Shuttle Relay
1. In partners, A stands approximately 30 feet opposite B. A runs and touches B's right shoulder. When B's shoulder is touched, B should run back to the starting line. Repeat five times.

2. In groups of four, repeat Task #1. A touches B's right shoulder. B touches C's right shoulder. C touches D's shoulder. Then D completes the last leg of the run. The relay starts and ends at the same line. Repeat five times.
3. Repeat Task #2 having the runners assume a crouch start position prior to being tagged.
4. Repeat Task #3 in a race against another shuttle relay team. Concentrate on staying in your lane.

Pursuit Relay

5. In partners, the passer (A) holds a baton in the left hand and brings it upward in an underhand motion into the palm (turned downward) of the receiver's (B) right hand. The receiver looks at the baton until it is grasped. Rotate and repeat the visual pass.
6. In partners, the passer (A) holds a baton in the left hand and brings it upward in an underhand motion into the "V" of the receiver's (B) right hand. The receiver does not turn to see the baton but accepts it looking straight ahead. Rotate and repeat the nonvisual pass.
7. In partners, without a baton, have the receiver (B) begin 15 feet ahead so that B can be moving forward as the passer (A) arrives. Tap the receiver's hand as a signal to go. Rotate and repeat.
8. Repeat Task #7 attempting to equalize the speeds of the incoming passer and the outgoing receiver. The receiver must be more sensitive to the passer's speed since passer will be fatigued. The passer can give a signal for the receiver to begin to run.
9. Repeat Task #8 with a baton using the visual pass. Repeat using a nonvisual pass.
10. Repeat Task #9 being certain to transfer the baton into the left hand after receiving it.
11. In groups of four, execute a relay team drill. The four team members stand at least 30 feet apart in a line so that B (first receiver) can be running as the baton is received from A. B (second runner) places the baton in the left hand and exchanges to C (third runner) who is also moving forward.C passes the baton to D (fourth runner). D runs 10 yards, turns around and carries the baton back to the start and becomes the new first passer. Use a visual pass for 10 minutes. Repeat using a nonvisual pass.
12. In groups of four, run a relay on an oval track carefully observing the 22-yard exchange zone. After passing the baton, be conscious of staying in the lane to avoid interfering with other team exchanges. Use the visual pass for two relays. Repeat using the nonvisual pass.

HURDLE

Purpose:
To leap over a hurdle or bar while sprinting or dashing.

Skill Analysis:
1. Move the arms in opposition to the legs.
2. Stretch the arms forward to get more lift.
3. Bend the knee of the trailing leg and point it to the side when going over the hurdle.
4. Bring the lead leg down to the ground fast when the hurdle is cleared.
5. Take an uneven number of steps between hurdles.

Task Learning Experiences:
1. Take a short run and leap.
2. Run ten yards, leap, run ten more yards, leap, run ten more yards, leap, etc.
3. Run alongside of the hurdles, taking a leap when opposite each hurdle.
4. Run alongside of the hurdles, allowing only the trailing leg to extend over the hurdle during each leap.

5. Run and hurdle over cones spread apart approximately every ten yards.
6. Run and hurdle over bars resting on the seats of chairs (18" high) approximately ten yards apart.
7. Run and hurdle over bars resting on the top of chairs (30" high) approximately ten yards apart.
8. Run and hurdle (actual hurdle) on grass—each hurdle being approximately ten yards apart.
9. Run and hurdle (actual hurdle) on grass with hurdles at proper distance (26'3" between each hurdle).
10. Run and hurdle on grass (proper distance) attempting to establish a consistent takeoff foot with three or five strides in-between.
11. Run and hurdle on track for entire distance of race.
12. Using a crouch start—spring and hurdle the entire distance of the race.
13. In groups of three, race against each other in a 50-yard hurdle race.

STANDING LONG JUMP

Purpose:
To gain maximum distance when executing a forward and upward jump from a stand.

Skill Analysis:
1. Begin with the feet parallel, the body crouched, the knees flexed, and the arms forward.
2. Swing the arms forward and backward to build momentum.
3. Jump at the end of the third rocking motion and push off from the toes.
4. Jump from both feet.
5. Pull the legs up close to the body, then extend the legs forward as the body leans forward.
6. Land with the body weight forward and swing the arms forward to avoid falling backward.

Task Learning Experiences:
1. Stand behind a line and jump forward.
2. Stand behind a line and jump forward and upward.
3. Stand behind a line and swing your arms forward and backward with your body crouched and knees flexed.
4. Repeat Task #3 attempting to jump forward and upward at the end of three arm swings.
5. Repeat Task #4 concentrating on falling forward and relaxing upon landing.

6. Repeat Task #5 jumping to hit a mark placed beyond the jumper's ability.
7. In groups of three, A and B hold a string 1½ feet away and 1½ feet high while C performs the standing long jump over it. Rotate after each partner takes six jumps.
8. Practice measuring four jumps. (For evaluating jumping skill quickly, place foot markers along the side of the pit or mat so jumps can be approximated.)
9. Take 10 jumps, marking the farthest. (In order to keep track of the farthest jump, mark the first jump along the edge of the pit or mat. If the jump is shorter next time, do not mark it. If the jump is farther, remove the earlier mark and replace it with the farther one. When all jumping is completed, the final mark is measured.)
10. In partners, each take three jumps seeing who jumps the farthest.

RUNNING LONG JUMP

Purpose:
To gain maximum distance when executing a forward and upward jump which is preceded by a run.

Skill Analysis:
1. Build maximum speed during the run.
2.. Focus the eyes to a distance point—never downward.
3. Takeoff from one foot.
4. Swing the arms and legs upward and forward.
5. Use a sitting position when in the air.
6. Reach forward upon landing.

Task Learning Experiences:
1. Stand behind a line and jump forward.
2. Stand behind a line and jump forward and upward.
3. Stand behind a line and jump to a line four feet away.
4. Stand behind a line and jump to a line a jump beyond a line four feet away.
5. Stand behind a line and jump over a string two feet away and two feet high.
6. Take a ten yard run and jump from one foot onto a mat, into a pit, or onto grass.
7. Take a ten-yard run and jump from one foot toward a colored mark (tape) onto the mat, pit, or grass.
8. Take a ten-yard run and jump from one foot over a string three feet away and two feet high.
9. Take a twenty-five yard run and jump from one foot.
10. Take a twenty-five yard run and jump from one foot attempting to grasp the knees while in the air.

11. Take a run in which maximum speed can be reached and jump from one foot concentrating on falling forward upon landing.
12. Take a run and sight a mark ahead in the distance before the jump from one foot.
13. For evaluating jumping skill, mark the first jump. If the jump is shorter the next time, do not mark it. If the jump is farther, remove the earlier mark and replace it with the farther one. When all jumping is completed, measure the final mark. Take ten jumps, marking the farthest.
14. In partners, take three jumps seeing who can jump the farthest.

HIGH JUMP

Purpose:
To gain maximum height over a bar when executing an upward jump.

Skill Analysis: Basic to All High Jumping
1. Use an approach in which the jumper reaches the takeoff point with the proper foot. This can be achieved by taking an odd

number of steps starting with the left (left foot takeoff) or right (right foot takeoff) foot.

2. Place the takeoff foot about an arm's distance from the bar so that the nonjumping foot can swing upward with the knee bent.
3. Lift the body over the bar so that no part of the body knocks the bar during the layout.
4. Land on the back or side depending on the jumping form employed. The most important point to remember in landing is to relax so the force will be absorbed.

Additional Skill Analyses:
Straddle Roll
1. Use a 35°-40° angle approach (run) to the bar.
2. Takeoff from the inside leg and thrust the lead leg upward.
3. Swing the arms upward to get more height before the layout.
4. Rotate the body to a face down position (stomach and head face the bar) during the layout.
5. Reach downward with the arm and shoulder on the other side of the bar to initiate the roll for the landing.
6. Land on the back or side of the body.

Back Flop (Fosbury)
1. Use a curved approach (run) in order to assist in rotating the body for the takeoff.
2. Takeoff from the outside foot and lift the inside knee up. (Be careful to take a one foot takeoff.)
3. Begin to rotate the body before the takeoff so the back is turned toward the bar as the body leaves the ground.
4. Extend the body and keep it horizontal while going over the bar backward.
5. Drop the head backward after clearing the bar so the hips will be lifted over the bar.
6. Land on the upper part of the back.

Task Learning Experiences:
Straddle Roll
1. Stand beside the bar (arm's length) and lift the nonjumping leg upward, taking a hop on the takeoff foot.
2. Take three steps from the side (35°-40° angle), place the takeoff foot beside the bar, lift the jumping leg upward while hopping on the takeoff foot.
3. Repeat Task #2 using seven running steps. Seven running steps is approximately twelve walking steps.
4. Execute the seven running step approach, takeoff, and then cross over a 2½ feet high string by lying face down (stomach and head face the string) followed by a landing on your side or back. (See Skill Analysis.)
5. Execute the straddle roll using a bar placed at 2½ feet.
6. Execute the straddle roll using a bar placed at three feet.

7. Repeat Task #6 adjusting the angle used on the approach to best clear the bar. (This may vary from 35° to 40°.)
8. Repeat Task #6 attempting to lean back during the takeoff rather than forward and concentrating on increasing arm uplift to gain height.
9. Raise the bar an inch after clearing three feet three times.
10. When maximum height is reached, lower the bar four inches in order to work on form without injury to the muscles.
11. At the end of the form practice, raise the bar two inches above the maximum height as a challenge to reach a higher goal.

Back Flop
12. Without a bar, stand beside the pit (where the bar would be) and swing the inside leg upward and push off with the outside leg. Land in a sitting position in the pit.
13. Repeat Task #12 lifting both legs high and falling on the back.
14. Repeat Task #13 concentrating on getting more height with the body before coming down into the pit.
15. Without a bar, take three steps from the side, takeoff and land backward in the pit.
16. Repeat Task #15 using a seven running steps curved approach. Curve toward the center after the third step.
17. Hold a string at approximately 2½ feet. Take the seven step curved approach and begin to rotate the body before the takeoff so the back is turned toward the string as the body leaves the ground. Land on the upper part of the back. (See Skill Analysis).
18. Repeat Task #17 keeping the body horizontal as it goes over the string backward.
19. Repeat Task #18 lowering the head after clearing the string so the hips are lifted over the string.

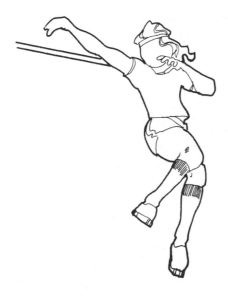

Back flop take off

20.   Repeat Task #19 using a bar placed at 2½ feet.
21.   Repeat Task #20 using a bar placed at three feet.
22.   Raise the bar an inch after clearing three feet three times.
23.   When maximum height is reached, lower the bar four inches in order to work on form without injury to the muscles.
24.   At the end of the form practice, raise the bar two inches above the maximum height as a challenge to reach a higher goal.

SOFTBALL THROW

Purpose:
To throw the softball forward and upward in order to gain the maximum distance.

Skill Analysis:
1.   Throw from either a stand or a run. However, the foot must not touch or cross over the throwing line.
2.   Hold the ball in the fingers (not palm).
3.   Keep the feet in a forward-back stride with weight on the rear foot just prior to the throw.
4.   Swing the arm back with a bent elbow and then lead with the elbow as the throwing arm moves forward and weight is transferred to the forward foot.
5.   Release the ball at a 45° angle and follow through with the throwing arm as a step forward is taken by the rear leg.

Task Learning Experiences:

1. Stand behind a line and throw a yarn ball or fleece ball as far as possible.
2. Repeat Task #1 making certain that the body is in a forward-backward stride and that the throwing arm moves forward with a bent elbow lead.
3. Repeat Task #2 concentrating on transferring the weight from the rear to the lead leg.
4. Continue to practice throwing from behind a line with the yarnball. Tie a six-inch string to the yarnball and the other end to the wrist so that the ball will not have to be retrieved each time.
5. Repeat Tasks #2 and #3, throwing a softball from behind a line.
6. Repeat Task #5 with a partner who will retrieve the ball and throw the ball back from an adjacent line.
7. Stand with your heels to the throwing line and take a five step run and hop as if about to throw. This is the point at which to start if throwing from a run.
8. With a starting point established for a throw from a run, take a run and throw a yarnball attached to the wrist (as in Task #4). Repeat until a smooth transition is established from the run to the hop to the throw.
9. Repeat Task #8 using a softball.
10. In partners, repeat Task #8 using a softball. A throws the ball from a run behind an adjacent line and B retrieves. Reverse.
11. In groups of three, A takes three throws allowing B to retrieve the ball. C then takes three throws while A takes B's place. Rotate.
12. In groups of five, compete to see who can throw the farthest. The best of three throws is the one which is counted in the competition. Mark the throws with stakes, measuring with a tape when all the throws are completed.

SHOT PUT
Purpose:
To push the shot forward and upward in order to gain maximum distance.

Skill Analysis:
1. Use a forward-backward stride with knees slightly bent in order to have a wide base of support.
2. Rest the shot on the fingertips close to the neck.
3. Keep the elbow bent and away from the body for leverage.
4. Apply force to the shot by extending first the legs, followed by extension of the arm.
5. Step forward with the rear foot in order to transfer the weight and gain momentum on the push.

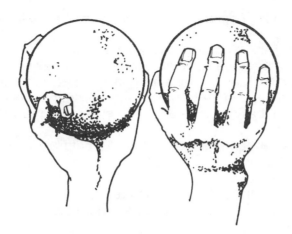

Three and four finger shot put grip

Task Learning Experiences:

1. Stand in a forward-backward stride and practice holding an imaginary shot concentrating on bending the elbow and resting the shot on the fingertips.
2. Practice an imaginary push extending the legs, then the arms.
3. Practice the footwork for a put from a stand. (Place footprints in a circle which can be followed to establish the footwork.)
4. Use a softball in place of the imaginary shot to practice the grip and push techniques.

5.   Combine the grip and push techniques with the footwork using the softball.
6.   Repeat Task #5 using a six-pound shot.
7.   Increase the speed of the footwork for more explosive strength.
8.   Practice the footwork for a put from a glide. (Place footprints in a circle which can be followed to establish the footwork.)
9.   Use a softball (in place of a shot) in order to practice the glide footwork.
10.   Using an 8-pound shot, execute the put from a glide.
11.   In groups of four, each student takes five puts. A puts, B evaluates the put, C measures the put, and D records the distance of the put. Rotate and repeat.
12.   In groups of five, compete to see who puts the farthest out of three trials.

DISCUS THROW

Purpose:
To propel the discus forward and upward in order to obtain maximum distance.

Skill Analysis:
1.   Use the standing throw in the first stages of learning.
2.   Spread the hand across the discus until the fingertips extend over the edge of the discus.
3.   Stand with the left side of the body facing the direction of the throw and swing the discus back and forth several times to build momentum.

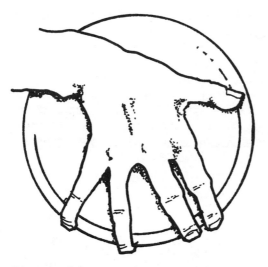

Discus grip

4. Transfer the body weight to the back foot, then to the forward foot to gain maximum force for the actual throw.
5. Extend the throwing arm back to waist height as far as possible, then start moving it forward behind the body so the transfer of weight of the body causes a whip.
6. Use a throw with a turn only when a high skill level is attained. If the turn is not executed properly, it will be less efficient than the standing throw.

Task Learning Experiences:
1. Hold a frisbee with the proper grip.
2. Stand in a forward-backward stride and swing the frisbee back and forth.
3. Practice the footwork for a throw from a stand. (Place footprints in a circle which can be followed to establish footwork.)
4. Throw the frisbee using the proper footwork and swing. The throwing arm extends back at waist height as far as possible, then starts forward behind the body. Transfer of weight from the left foot to the right foot, then to the left foot again, causes a whip.
5. Repeat Task #4 taking two preliminary swings prior to the throw to build momentum.
6. Repeat Task #5 using a standard 2-lb. 3-oz. discus which is taped to the hand so it is not released or dropped. This provides practice in the preliminary swings as well as the footwork without having to concentrate on direction and distance of the discus.
7. Repeat Task #6 without taping the discus to the hand. Remember safety precautions so other students are not hit with the discus.

8. Repeat Task #7 observing the competitive rules:
   8.1 Throw between a 60° sector.
   8.2 Do not touch any part of your body on or outside the circle until the throw is marked.
   8.3 Leave the circle from the rear half.
9. In groups of four, each student takes five discus throws. A throws, B evaluates the throw, C marks the throw, and D measures and records the distance of the throw with C's assistance. Rotate and repeat. (Only mark and measure the farthest throw of the five.)
10. In groups of five, each student takes three discus throws and competes to see who throws the farthest.

FIFTEEN

Tumbling

BODY SHAPES

Purpose:

To recognize basic body shapes and incorporate them into symmetrical and asymmetrical positions.

Skill Analysis: Definitions
1. A symmetrical shape is when body parts on both sides of the body match in position in space.
2. An asymmetrical shape is when a body part does not match spatially the corresponding part on the opposite side of the body.
3. The base of support consists of the part or parts of the body over which the center of gravity is balanced.

Task Learning Experiences:
1. Support your weight or center of gravity on three bases of support or body parts.
2. Support your weight on two bases or parts. Try combining two different body parts.
3. Balance the center of gravity over one base for support. How many different single bases of support can you find and still maintain balance?
4. Support your weight on four bases of support. Try other combinations of four bases.
5. Make a round shape with the body.
6. Transfer the center of gravity from one base of support to another without destroying the flow of the movement while in the round shape.

7. Assume the following shapes with the body:
   7.1 Straight.
   7.2 Narrow.
   7.3 Angular.
   7.4 Twisted.
   7.5 Wide.
8. Repeat Task #7 performing each body shape using a different base of support each time.
9. Combine three movements together into a sequence or routine. Perform a locomotor skill, a shape in the air, and conclude with a balanced position. Repeat combining 3 different movements.
10. Make a symmetrical shape with the body.
11. Make a wide symmetrical shape.
12. Make a narrow symmetrical shape.
13. Make an asymmetrical shape.
14. Make a twisted asymmetrical shape.
15. In partners, A "mirrors" B's shape. Repeat changing:
    15.1 Shape.
    15.2 Base of support.
    15.3 Symmetrical position.
    15.4 Asymmetrical position.
16. In groups of three or four, make an obstacle course where the body must change shape while moving in space. (Use equipment which the teacher makes available.)

ROLLS

Purpose:
To perform various rolls which are initiated with the hands supporting the weight of the body and then weight is transferred from one body part to another while moving across the mat.

Skill Analysis:
1. Transfer weight from one body part to another in a sequential pattern.

Forward roll in three stages

2. Use the hands to support the weight of the body for all curl-shaped rolls.
3. Have a beginning and an ending to all rolls.

Kinds: Forward, backward, straddle, egg, backward extension

Task Learning Experiences:
1. Roll the body across the mat, transferring weight from one body part to another, never moving back to the previous body part.
2. Repeat Task #1 rolling in another direction.
3. Starting from a low curled position (hands on mat and weight supported by the feet), move in a forward direction transferring weight from one body part to another. This is called a forward roll. Repeat three times.
4. Repeat Task #3 beginning and ending in a standing narrow shape.
5. Repeat Task #4 performing a succession of three rolls.
6. Repeat Task #3 changing the lower half of the body from a curled to a wide shape halfway through, thus completing the roll in a standing straddle shape. Push up using the hands on the inside of the legs.
7. Repeat Task #6 performing a succession of three straddle rolls. Move from the wide shape back into the curled shape to begin each forward roll.
8. Do a forward roll with the legs in a crossed position. Do a succession of three rolls in this position.
9. Beginning in a squat position, roll backward placing the hands on each side of the head. Repeat three times.
10. Repeat Task #9 attempting to return to the feet in a squat position without rolling over (rocking motion). This is an egg roll.
11. Repeat Task #9 attempting to push with the hands as they are placed beside the head and thus rolling completely over to the squat position again. This is called a backward roll.
12. Try a succession of three backward rolls, beginning on the feet in a squat position and ending on the feet. Concentrate on pushing with the hands as they are placed to each side of the head.
13. From a standing position, begin the backward roll and halfway through change the lower part of your body to a wide shape ending on the feet. This is a straddle backward roll. Repeat three times.
14. Repeat Task #11 extending the legs straight into the air (instead of remaining curled) as the hands push next to the head. The resulting position after rolling over will be a stand. This is called a backward extension roll. Repeat three times.
15. Combine several different rolls while moving down the mat. Choice of rolls include: forward roll, straddle forward roll, egg roll, backward roll, straddle backward roll, backward roll extension.
16. Combine several rolls with several balances to create a routine.
17. Demonstate the routine from Task #16 to the rest of the class.

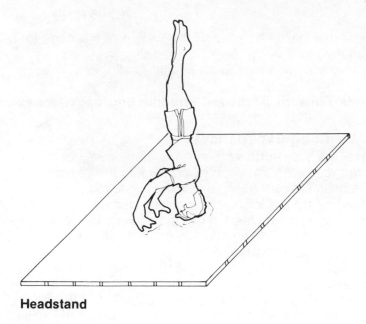

Headstand

HEADSTAND

Purpose:
To support the body in an inverted balanced position on the hands and head.

Skill Analysis:
1. Place the hands and head in a triangle with the hands shoulder-width apart and the head an equal distance from the hands.
2. Point the hands forward and spread the fingers.
3. Place the weight on the front of the head.
4. Point the toes while in the inverted position.

Task Learning Experiences[1]:
1. Perform a tripod and hold for five seconds. (A tripod is a balance on the head and hands with the knees resting on the elbows.) Repeat three times.
2. Hold a tripod with the knees lifted off the elbows and close to the chest for five seconds. Repeat three times.
3. From a tripod, extend the legs upward into a headstand and hold for five seconds. Dismount by lowering the legs. Repeat five times.
4. Repeat Task #1 doing a forward roll out of the tripod.
5. Repeat Task #3 doing a forward roll out of the headstand.
6. Begin a headstand in a flat, prone position and slowly pull the body up into a balanced headstand. Hold five seconds. The legs remain straight during the entire skill. Repeat three times.
7. Hold the headstand five seconds and position the legs in a straddle. Repeat three times.

1. For the "Headstand" and all succeeding tumbling skills, the use of spotters is advised.

8. Hold the headstand five seconds and position the legs in a forward-backward stride. Repeat three times.
9. Hold the headstand and rotate the body halfway around while maintaining the inverted position.
10. Repeat Task #9 moving in a full circle.
11. From a headstand, extend the arms and lift the body into a handstand. Hold three seconds, tuck the head, and roll out. Repeat three times.
12. Combine two rolls with the headstand to create a movement sequence.
13. Combine several tumbling skills with the headstand in order to create a routine.

CARTWHEEL

Purpose:
To change the base of support from one hand to the other, then one foot to the other foot.

Skill Analysis:
1. Support the body weight with only one body part at a time.
2. Transfer weight from one hand to the other hand, then one foot to the other foot.
3. Focus the eyes on the hands as the body is inverted.
4. Perform the cartwheel in a straight line.
5. Reach a full extension of the body while performing the skill.

Task Learning Experiences:
1. With the side facing the direction of intended movement, place the nearest hand and then the other hand on the mat, swinging

your hips over as you place the hands. You will land in a squat position. Repeat several times.

2. Place one hand and then the other onto the mat but this time push off from the mat with slightly bent knees and extend the legs over the hips. Land as straight as possible. Repeat five times.
3. Repeat Task #2 concentrating on moving in a straight pathway.
4. Perform three cartwheels in succession. Repeat three times.
5. Perform three cartwheels extending the distances between the hands and feet. This will prolong the length of the cartwheel. Repeat three times.
6. In partners and facing each other, perform a cartwheel together. Repeat, performing a succession of three cartwheels.
7. Perform a left side cartwheel reverse, and perform a right side cartwheel.
8. Perform a delayed cartwheel (dive). This is the same as the cartwheel except for an extension of the arms and torso into the air prior to contacting the floor. Repeat three times.
9. Perform a cartwheel using only one hand (lead hand) to support the weight of the body. Repeat three times.
10. Combine a cartwheel with other tumbling skills to create a routine.

HANDSTAND

Purpose:
To maintain balance while supporting the center of gravity over the hands.

Handstand to forward roll

Skill Analysis:
1. Align the body parts to maintain balance while in the inverted position.
2. Focus the eyes ahead and hold the head up while in the inverted position.
3. Point the toes while in the inverted position.
4. Shift the hands slightly if necessary to maintain balance.
5. Avoid too much arch in the back (banana handstand).

Task Learning Experiences:
1. In groups of three A executes a kick-up handstand against a wall while B and C assist. A takes a step forward and reaches toward the floor with the hands (shoulder-width apart) while kicking up with the rear foot. This is followed by kicking up with the remaining leg thus initiating the inverted balance. To dismount, reverse the above. Rotate. Repeat five times holding the handstand three seconds.
2. Repeat Task #1 away from a wall.
3. Kick up into a balanced handstand and hold for five counts. This should be done on a mat.
4. Repeat Task #3 until successful five times.
5. While holding a handstand position, slightly overbalance, slowly bend the arms and flex the hips, bringing the legs down to the body. Tuck the head and begin a forward roll from the shoulders. Try to do this successfully several times holding the handstand three seconds.
6. Begin as in a cartwheel but hold the handstand position with the feet together. Arch the back and go into a back walkover. (Arch the back, dropping the feet to the mat and then arch up to a stand.) Repeat three times.
7. Combine several tumbling skills with the handstand in order to create a routine.

8. Perform a handstand and move forward. Try walking on the hands for two feet, three feet, five feet.
9. From a handstand try walking on the hands and changing directions.
10. Combine tumbling skills with walking on the hands in order to create a routine.
11. From a headstand, extend (push upward) the arms into a handstand. Hold three seconds, tuck the head, and roll out. Repeat three times.
12. Combine a headstand into a handstand with other skills in order to create a routine.

FRONT WALKOVER

Purpose:
To change the base of support from feet to hands and back to feet in a forward direction while rotating the center of gravity over the base of support.

Skill Analysis:
1. Take a standing position and reach forward to the floor with both hands.
2. Kick up one leg and follow with a push off and kick with the other leg to an inverted position.
3. Continue moving the first leg over from the vertical position until that foot touches the floor.
4. Arch the back into a backbend position when the first foot reaches the floor.
5. Push off simultaneously with the arms in order to bring the other foot over to the floor.
6. Return to a vertical stand.

Task Learning Experiences:
1. Perform a backbend by pushing the back into an arch from a supine position. Push with the hands and legs. Hold for five seconds. Repeat five times.
2. Perform a backbend by first executing a handstand and then bringing both legs over to the floor to form an arch with the back. Hold five seconds. Repeat five times.
3. Perform a front walkover, concentrating on bringing over one leg at a time while inverted. (See Skill Analysis for step-by-step instruction.) Repeat 10 times.
4. Attempt to perform two front walkovers in succession. Repeat three times.
5. Try five front walkovers in succession.
6. Perform a front walkover and switch legs while inverted. Repeat three times.

7. Perform a front walkover and scissor the legs while inverted. Repeat three times.
8. Maintain the hands in the inverted position for a count of five before finishing the front walkover.
9. Combine the front walkover with two other skills into a routine.
10. Perform a movement sequence combining a cartwheel, headstand, handstand, and a front walkover.

BACK WALKOVER

Purpose:
To change the base of support from feet to hands and back to feet in a backward direction while rotating the center of gravity over the seat of support.

Skill Analysis:
1. Reach backward to the floor with the hands.
2. Point the fingers toward the feet.
3. Gather momentum by shifting the center of gravity over the hands while the leg kicks.
4. Position the head back so that the eyes can eventually focus on the floor.
5. Continue the momentum by bringing the rear leg over to a standing position.

Task Learning Experiences:
1. Begin a supine position with the back to the floor with the hands on each side of the head and the feet placed near the hips, push up into a backbend. Hold for five seconds. Repeat five times.
2. Assuming a backbend position, rock back and forth, trying to force the shoulders forward. Rock five times. Repeat three times.
3. Walk in the backbend position in a forward direction for five steps. Repeat in a backward direction for five steps.
4. Perform a backbend by reaching backward from a standing position. Repeat three times.
5. Stand facing a wall about one and one-half feet away. Bend into a backbend and lift one foot until the foot is flat against the wall. Support the body with the hands and the one foot that is against the wall and lead the body with the other leg over to a standing position. Repeat five times.
6. Stand and perform a backbend lifting the lead leg over to a standing position without the aid of the wall. (For students having difficulty, get into groups of three. A and B assist C in lifting the lead leg over. Rotate.) Repeat 10 times.
7. Perform two back walkovers in succession.
8. Perform a back walkover and switch the legs while inverted. Repeat three times.

9. Perform a back walkover and scissor the legs while inverted. Repeat three times.
10. Combine the back walkover with a cartwheel and front walkover.
11. Combine the back walkover with other tumbling skills to create a routine.

ROUTINES—FLOOR EXERCISE[1]

Purpose:
To perform a combination of tumbling skills in such a way that they flow smoothly, continuously, and rhythmically from one to another.

Skill Analysis:
1. Choose tumbling skills on a basis of quality of flow with the previous skill as well as the skill to follow.
2. Begin and end each routine with a held (static) position.
3. Plan routines with changes in direction, levels, and pathways.
4. Practice a routine exactly the same each time in order to develop perfection and precision.

Task Learning Experiences:
1. Choose a static position with which the routine will begin. It must be balanced. Hold the position five seconds. Repeat three times.
2. In choosing the first tumbling skill, consider the following questions:
   2.1 Is there flow from the static position to the beginning of the skill?
   2.2 How much space will you consume on your pathway?
   2.3 How many times will you repeat the skill?
3. Practice moving from the static position into performance of the skill itself.
4. In selecting the second skill consider items 2.1 through 2.3 in Task #2 and attempt to change the level or direction from the first skill.
5. Continue developing the routine until you have combined five skills. (Remember to begin and end the routine with a static position.)
6. After choosing the pathways the routine will follow, walk through them until they are established mentally.
7. Practice the entire routine.
8. Combine the entire routine to music.
9. Videotape the routine in order to evaluate your performance. Then play the videotape for a partner to evaluate.
10. Demonstrate the routine to the rest of the class.

1. NOTE: "Floor Exercise" is basically the incorporation of tumbling skills into a routine although it is considered an integral part of "Gymnastics."

SIXTEEN

Volleyball

CHEST PASS — OVERHAND VOLLEY

Purpose:
To receive the service and to send the ball to the set passer. The chest pass might also be used to send the ball over the net if the set passer cannot receive the ball or if it cannot be spiked.

Skill Analysis:
1. Use a forward-backward stride with bent knees.
2. Flex the elbows.
3. Hold the hands just below the chin with the fingers facing upward and backward.
4. Push with the fingers and straighten the elbows upward and forward when contacting the ball.
5. Extend the body upward on contact.
   Follow through upward and forward in the direction of intended flight.
7. Squat when necessary to avoid lifting a low ball.

Task Learning Experiences:
1. Place hands and body in a chest pass position and move as if hitting an imaginary ball.
2. Throw a balloon into the air and execute the chest pass whenever it reaches chin level.
3. Throw a beachball[1] into the air and use a chest pass to send the ball toward a wall. Chest pass the rebounds.

1. A colorful playball can be substituted for a beachball and, in some instances, may be preferable.

4. Repeat Task #3 executing as many chest passes as possible in a 30-second time period.
5. In partners, repeat Task #3 sending to a partner instead of a wall. Reverse and repeat.
6. In partners, execute 10 chest passes volleying from a distance of 10 feet. Increase the distance to 15 feet. Increase to 20 feet.
7. In groups of five, A tosses the beachball up and executes a chest pass to any of the four students grouped in a circle. The receiver uses a chest pass to send the ball to another, etc. Attempt to keep the ball in play as long as possible.
8. Repeat Task #7 keeping the ball in play 30 seconds, one minute, two minutes.
9. In partners, A tosses the beachball into air and uses the chest pass to send the ball to B over a 20-foot rope extended horizontally across the gymnasium. Reverse. (Height is necessary in the chest pass so that the set passer can retrieve it.)
10. In groups of four, A tosses the beachball to self and executes a chest pass to B. B set passes to C. C spikes the beachball over the net to D who retrieves the ball. Rotate and repeat 10 times.
11. Repeat Task #10 with D attempting to block the spiked ball.
12. Repeat Tasks #1-#11 using a volleyball.

SET PASS—OVERHEAD VOLLEY

Purpose:
To position the ball for another player to spike.

Skill Analysis:
1. Use a forward-backward stride with bent knees.
2. Flex the knees and elbows prior to the hit.
3. Tilt the head back.
4. Form a window with the hands above the face.
5. Watch the ball closely.
6. Hit the ball with the fingertips in an upward and forward direction.
7. Extend the body upward on contact.
8. Follow through in the direction of intended flight.

Task Learning Experiences:
1. Throw a beachball in the air and set pass. Concentrate on the Skill Analysis.
2. Execute consecutive set passes.
3. Repeat Task #2 ten consecutive times, 15 consecutive times.
4. Repeat Task #2 moving through space while set passing.
5. In partners, A tosses the Ball to B who set passes. Concentrate on getting below the ball and extending the body upward on contact. Reverse and repeat.

Set pass—overhead volley

6. Repeat Task #5 set passing ten consecutive times, 15 consecutive times.
7. Repeat Task #5 moving through space.
8. Throw a beachball against a wall and set pass the ball on the rebound.
9. In partners, A volleys a beachball against the wall; then B set passes the rebounding ball. Reverse and repeat.
10. In groups of six, circle set pass. Players set pass the beachball to anyone in the circle as many times as possible without allowing the ball to hit the floor.
11. Repeat Task #10 changing direction often. For more challenge, add another ball.
12. In partners, A set passes the beachball to B over a 12-foot rope extended horizontally across gymnasium. (This is used in order to achieve height in volleying.) Continue back and forth for five minutes.
13. Repeat Task #12 set passing ten consecutive times.
14. In groups of three, A chest passes to B; B set passes to C; C spikes the beachball.
15. Repeat Task #14 using a net. The net may be kept lower than standard if the students are younger. If a net is not available, a rope or ribbon extended horizontally across the gymnasium may be used.
16. Repeat Tasks #1-#15 using a volleyball.
17. Repeat Tasks #9-#16 using a backward set pass by tilting the head back and arching the body.

UNDERHAND SERVE

Purpose:
To put the ball into play by sending the ball over the net.

Skill Analysis:
1. Use a forward-backward stride with bent knees.
2. Hold the ball in the left hand across and in front of the body.
3. Swing arm back and hit the ball off the hand.
4. Transfer weight from the rear foot to the forward foot.
5. Contact the ball with the heel of the hand.
6. Follow through in the direction of intended flight.

Task Learning Experiences:
1. Facing a wall, bounce a beachball to the side and strike it forward and upward from underneath with the heel of the hand.
2. Facing a wall, strike (serve) a beachball out of the hand in a forward and upward direction several times.
3. Serve a beachball aiming above a 6-foot line on a wall. (Higher for older students).
4. Repeat Task #3 contacting the ball on different surfaces. Adjust the ball holding hand at various heights. What happens to the flight pattern?
5. In partners, A serves a beachball to B who is approximately 20 feet away.
6. Repeat Task #5 from a distance of 30 feet.
7. Serve a beachball over the net into the opposite court from a point halfway between the serving line and net.
8. Mark a volleyball court as diagrammed. Serve the beachball five times attempting to make the ball land in the high scoring zone. Stand halfway between serving line and net.

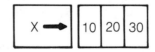

9. Repeat Tasks #1-#8 using a volleyball.
10. Repeat Tasks #7 and #8 using the actual serving line and a volleyball.
11. Serve a volleyball to the right back position. Complete one out of five, 3/5, 4/5.
12. Serve a volleyball to the left back position. Complete one out of five, 3/5, 4/5.
13. Serve a volleyball to the right forward position. Complete one out of five, 3/5, 4/5.
14. Serve a volleyball to the left forward position. Complete one out of five, 3/5, 4/5.
15. In a game situation, serve the ball to the open spots or to the far corners.

OVERHAND SERVE

Purpose:
To put the ball in play by sending it on a horizontal plane across the net (no arc).

Skill Analysis:
1. Take a forward-backward stride position with the knees slightly flexed.
2. Toss the ball about three feet above the shoulder so the hand can meet the ball just above head height.
3. Transfer weight from the rear foot to the forward foot as the ball is contacted.
4. Contact the ball with the heel of the hand as the hand forms a fist.
5. Extend the elbow and flex the wrist forward as the ball is contacted.
6. Follow through in the direction of the intended flight and then swing downward.

Task Learning Experiences:

NOTE: Lower the net according to age, grade level, and/or skill ability.

1. Stand with the body in a forward-backward stride position, toss an imaginary ball into the air, bring the fist overhead and imitate the striking and follow-through of the volleyball with the heel on the hand.
2. Take a beachball and practice tossing the ball approximately three feet into the air over the forward shoulder.
3. Take a forward-backward stride position about ten feet from a wall. Toss the beachball into the air and contact the ball with heel of the hand. The hit (serve) must be a quick, short contact.
4. Repeat Task #3 aiming above a 6-foot line on the wall. (Higher for older students.)
5. Repeat Task #4 placing a second line parallel to and three feet above the original line. Complete 10 serves between the lines.
6. In partners, using the overhand serve, A serves the beachball to B who is 30 feet away. Try to maintain a horizontal flight. Reverse and repeat 5 times.
7. In partners, standing at opposite midcourts, A and B execute the overhand serve back and forth with a beachball or playball.
8. Repeat Task #7 standing behind the serving line near the center of the court. This allows for a margin of error in a right or left direction.
9. Repeat Tasks #2-#8 using a volleyball.
10. Divide the court into four zones. (One point for zone next to net,

two points for next zone, etc.) In partners, A serves the volleyball five times attempting to make the ball land in the high scoring zone. Two points are deducted if the serve is out of bounds or illegal. B retrieves the ball and rolls it under the net. After five tries, reverse and repeat.

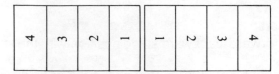

11. Practice overhand serve placement (around the clock). Serve to the position until successful:
    11.1 Serve to right back position.
    11.2 Serve to center back position.
    11.3 Serve to left back position.
    11.4 Serve to left forward position.
    11.5 Serve to center forward position.
    11.6 Serve to right forward position.
12. Concentrate on serving to the open spots during a game situation. If there are no open spaces, serve to the far corners.

DIG PASS (BUMP)

Purpose:
To return a ball that is received waist high or lower. It is especially useful when receiving a spike.

Skill Analysis:
1. Use a forward-backward stride with bent knees and waist.
2. Clench the fingers and turn the palms upward.
3. Keep the forearms, wrists, and elbows straight.
4. Contact the ball with an upward motion.
5. Extend the body when contacting the ball.
6. Follow through in the direction of the intended flight.

Task Learning Experiences:
1. Place hands and body in the dig pass position and move as if hitting an imaginary ball.
2. Use a balloon and execute the dig pass whenever it falls to waist level.
3. In partners, A hits a dig pass with the balloon to B. B returns the balloon to A with a dig pass.
4. Repeat Tasks #1-#3 using a beachball.
5. In partners, A tosses a beachball high into the air and B dig passes. After five dig passes, reverse.
6. Use a beachball and execute the dig pass against a wall several times. Concentrate on extending the body on contact.

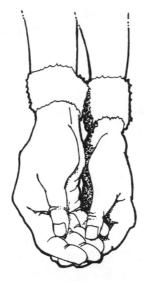

Hand position for dig or bump pass

7. In partners, A stands on a chair across the net and throws the beachball downward to B who is prepared to execute a dig pass. Reverse.
8. Repeat Tasks #5, #6, and #7 using a volleyball. (The volleyball can be slightly deflated if students are not ready for a hard ball.)
9. In groups of three, A throws the volleyball to B at waist height who then uses a dig pass to send the ball back over the net to the back court to C who retrieves the ball and rolls it back. Rotate positions and repeat.
10. Repeat Task #9, A volleying the ball to B instead of throwing.
11. In a game situation, enforce the rule that the third teammate to play the ball on a side must hit over the net using a dig pass.

SPIKE (OFFENSIVE TIP)

Purpose:
To direct the ball downward across the net in the form of a smash. This is an offensive technique.

Skill Analysis:
1. Be ready for the spike by facing the direction of the ball, placing the weight forward, and preparing the leap.
2. Takeoff for the jump from one foot.
3. Turn the body to the side in midair.
4. Contact the ball at the highest possible point.
5. Contact the ball with a stiff arm, quick flexion of the wrist.
6. Strike the ball on the top so the flight is downward.

Task Learning Experiences:
1. Jump vertically taking off from one foot.
2. Jump vertically and turn the body to its side while in midair.
3. Jump vertically and as the body is turned, extend the arm into the air.
4. Stand beside the net, jump, turn body, and extend the arm closest to the net imitating a downward hit. Repeat several times.
5. Stand next to the net, toss a beachball into the air, jump, and spike it. Repeat five times.
6. In partners, A holds a beachball just above the net by standing on a chair and allows B to improve timing by jumping and spiking it. Reverse.
7. In groups of three, A stands to the side and tosses a beachball high to B who is close to the net for the spike. C retrieves the spike. Rotate positions and repeat.
8. Repeat Tasks #5, #6 and #7 with a volleyball (deflate slightly if needed).
9. In a game situation, enforce the rule that the third teammate to play the ball on a side must hit over the net using a spike. The ball must be set up high and close to the net for the third player to spike.

BLOCK

Purpose:

To make the ball rebound over the net or to deflect the ball to a teammate. This is a defensive technique used against the spike.

Skill Analysis:
1. Stand close to the net.
2. Jump up to meet the ball as spiker jumps.
3. Thrust the arms forward and upward.
4. Hold the fingers tense and straight for rebound purposes.
5. Do not swing the arms forward as the body comes down. (A net foul could result.)

Task Learning Experiences:
1. Jump vertically as high as possible.
2. Jump vertically and concentrate on thrusting arms forward and upward.
3. Jump vertically, thrusting arms forward and upward and concentrate on holding fingers tense and straight. Repeat several times.
4. Repeat Task #3 standing beside a net to become aware of the height that is necessary to make the block.

5. Repeat Task #3 standing beside a net concentrating on not contacting the net as the body and arms descend.
6. In partners, A stands opposite B (across net). A jumps up imitating a spike while B jumps to imitate a block. Practice to improve blocking reaction time. Reverse.
7. Toss a beachball high against the wall, jump, and block the rebound.
8. In partners, A throws a beachball forcefully across the top of the net by standing on a chair. B must block the beachball. Reverse.
9. In groups of three, A stands to the side and tosses a beachball to B who is close to the net in order to spike. C blocks the spike. Rotate positions and repeat.
10. Repeat Tasks #7, #8, and #9 using a volleyball.
11. Repeat Tasks #8 and #9 using a volleyball and concentrate on deflecting the ball backward to a teammate rather than making the ball rebound back over the net.
12. In a game situation, alternate the uses of the block. At times, make the ball bounce back over the net and at other times deflect the ball to a teammate.

References

Ausubel, D.P. (1968). *Educational psychology a cognitive review.* New York: Holt, Rinehart & Winston.

Bailey, L. (1981). Systematic observation of activities in physical education: Need for research. *Physical Education Review, 4*(2), 96-102.

Banathy, B.H. (1968). *Instructional systems,* Palo Alto, CA: F.P. Fearon.

Becker, W.C., Engelmann, S., Carnine, D.W., & Rhine, W.R. (1981). The direct instruction model. In W.R. Rhine (Ed.), *Encouraging change in America's schools: A decade of experimentation.* New York: Academic Press.

Bell, V.L. (1970). *Sensorimotor learning.* Pacific Palisades, CA: Goodyear.

Berliner, D.C., & Rosenshine, B.U. (1977). The acquisition of knowledge in the classroom. In R.C. Anderson, R.J. Spiro, & W.E. Montague (Eds), *Schooling and the acquisition of knowledge.* Hillsdale, NJ: Erlbaum Press.

Bigge, M.L. (1964). *Learning theories for teachers.* New York: Harper and Row.

Blake, O.W., & Volp, A.M. (1964). *Lead-up games to team sports.* Englewood Cliffs, NJ: Prentice-Hall.

Bloss, M.V., & Brown, V.A. (1975). *Badminton.* Dubuque, IA: Wm. C. Brown.

Bompa, T. (1975). *Modern rhythmic gymnastics.* Modern Rhythmic Gymnastics Seminar, York University Department of Physical Education and Athletics.

Broer, M. (1969). *Efficiency for human movement.* Philadelphia: W.B. Saunders.

Bruner, J. (1961). The act of discovery. *Harvard Educational Review, 31,* 21-32.

Casady, D.R. (1974). *Sports activities for men.* New York: Macmillan.

Cooper, P. (1971). *Feminine gymnastics.* Minneapolis: Burgess.

Dauer, V. (1972). *Essential movement experience for preschool and primary children.* Minneapolis: Burgess.

Driver, H. (1973). *Tennis for teachers.* Madison, WI: Mona-Driver Book Company.

Drury, B. J. & Schmid, A.B. (1970). *Gymnastics for women.* Palo Alto, CA: National Press Books.

Ebert, F.H., & Cheatum, B.A. (1977). *Basketball.* Philadelphia: W.B. Saunders.

Eble, K. (1976). *The craft of teaching.* San Francisco: Jossey-Bass.

Exploration of basic movements in physical education. (1960). Detroit: Detroit Public Schools.

Fait, H. (1976). *Experiences in movement.* Philadelphia: W.B. Saunders.

Faulkner, E., & Weymuller, V. (1974). *Ed Faulkner's tennis.* New York: Dell.

Fielding, G.D., Kameenui, E., & Gersten, R. (1983, May/June). A comparison of an inquiry and a direct instruction approach to teaching legal concepts and applications to secondary school students. *Journal of Educational Research, 76*(5), 287-293.

Frederick, A.B. (1969). *Gymnastics for men.* Dubuque, IA: Wm. C. Brown.

Frederick, A.B. (1966). *Gymnastics for women.* Dubuque, IA: Wm. C. Brown.

Gage, N.L. (1972). *Teacher effectiveness and teacher education.* Palo Alto, CA: Pacific Books.

Gage, N.L. (1978). *The scientific basis of the art of teaching.* New York: Teacher's College Press.

Gagne, R.M. (1971). Learning research and its implications for independent learning. In R.A. Weisgerber (Ed.), *Perspectives in individualized learning* Palo Alto, CA: F.E. Peacock.

Gagne, R.M. (1970). *The conditions of learning.* New York: Holt, Rinehart & Winston.

Gensemer, R. (1975). *Tennis.* Philadelphia: W.B. Saunders.

Gilliom, B.C. (1970). *Basic movement education for children.* Reading, MA: Addison-Wesley.

Good, T.L. (1979, March/April). Teacher effectiveness in the elementary school. *Journal of Teacher Education,* **30**(2). 52-64.

Graham, G., & Heimerer, E. (1981). Research on teacher effectiveness: A summary with implications for teaching. *Quest,* **33**(1), 14-25.

Hackett, L.C., & Jensen, R.G. (1968). *A guide to movement exploration.* Palo Alto, CA: Peek Publications.

Hall, J.T., Lersten, K.C., Melnick, M.J., Morash, T.W., Perry, R.H., Pestolesk, R.A., & Seidler, B. (1969). *Fundamentals of physical education.* Pacific Palisades, CA: Goodyear.

Hill, W.F. (1971). *Learning: A survey of psychological interpretations.* Scranton, PA: Chandler.

Hudgins, B.B. (1971). *The instructional process.* Chicago: Rand McNally & Co.

Kirchner, G. (1974). *Physical education for elementary school children.* Dubuque, IA: Wm. C. Brown.

Kruger, H., & Kruger, J.M. (1977). *Movement education in physical education.* Dubuque, IA: Wm C. Brown.

Lawther, J.D. (1968). *The learning of physical skills.* Englewood Cliffs, NJ: Prentice-Hall.

Leighton, J. (1969). *Inside tennis: Techniques of winning.* Englewood Cliffs, NJ: Prentice-Hall.

Meyer, H., & Schwartz, M.M. (1966). *Team sports for girls and women.* Philadelphia: W.B. Saunders.

Mosston, M. (1966). *Teaching physical education.* Columbus, OH: Charles E. Merrill.

Mueller, R. (1976). Task cards in AAHPER (Ed.). *Personalized learning in physical education.* Washington, D.C., NEA, 1976.

Murphy, C., & Murphy, B. (1975). *Tennis for the player, teacher, and coach.* Philadelphia: W.B. Saunders.

Netcher, J.R. (1976, June). A learning system: What is it, why is it, how does it work? *Journal of Physical Education and Recreation,* **46**(6), 29-30.

Oliver, B. (1983). Direct instruction: An instructional model from a process-product study. In T.J. Templin & J.K. Olson (Eds.), *Teaching in physical education* (pp. 298-309). Champaign, IL: Human Kinetics.

Poole, J. (1973). *Badminton.* Pacific Palisades, CA: Goodyear.

Rink, J.E. (1981, February). The teacher wants us to learn. *Journal of Physical Education and Recreation,* **53**(2), 17-18.

Rosenshine, B.U. (1979). Content, time and direct instruction. In P. Peterson & H.F. Walberg (Eds.), *Research on teaching: Concepts, findings, and implications* Berkeley, CA: McCutchan.

Scates, A.E. (1973, October) Power volleyball. *Journal of Health, Physical Education and Recreation,* **44**(8), 32-39.

Schurr, E.L. (1967). *Movement experience for children.* New York: Appleton, Century, Crofts.

Scott, P.M., & Crafts, V.R. (1964). *Track and field for girls and women.* New York: Appleton, Century, Crofts.

Singer, R.N., & Dick, W. (1974). *Teaching physical education: A systems approach.* Boston: Houghton Mifflin.

Sjursen, H.S. (1968). *Girls' gymnastic workbook for physical educators.* Waldwick, NJ: Hocktor Records.

Thigpen, J. (1967). *Power volleyball for girls and women.* Dubuque, IA: Wm. C. Brown.

Vannier, M., & Poindexter, H.B. (1969). *Physical education activities for college women.* Philadelphia: W.B. Saunders.

Wakefield, F., Harkins, D., & Cooper, J.M. (1977). *Track and field fundamentals for girls and women.* St. Louis: The C. V. Mosby Co.

Weisgerber, R.A. (1971). *Developmental efforts in individualized learning.* Itasca, Illinois: F.E. Peacock.

Wickstrom, R.L. (1977). *Fundamental motor patterns.* Philadelphia: Lea & Febiger.

Wilkes, G. (1977). *Basketball for men.* Dubuque, IA: Wm. C. Brown.

Wilkinson, B. (1967). *Modern physical fitness.* New York: Viking Press.

Xanthos, P., & Johnson, J. (1972). *Tennis.* Dubuque, IA: Wm. C. Brown.

Zakrajsek, D., Carnes, L., & Leaf, B. (1976). *Physical education task pak.* Kent, OH: Cricket Press.

Zakrajsek, D., & Carnes, L. (1981). *Learning experiences: An approach to teaching physical education.* Dubuque, IA: Wm. C. Brown.

51